DEAR JOHN

Life Changing Love Letters to a Prisoner

*Written to Johnny L. Ellis
by Abraham Rose*

His Rose

His Rose, Inc.
Naperville, IL 60563-2534
www.hisrose.org

Dear John
Life Changing Love Letters to a Prisoner
Copyright © 2011 by His Rose, Inc.
All rights reserved

ISBN Number: 978-0-9789461-4-2
Library of Congress Control Number: 2011905238

Cover Design
    Abraham Rose

Publisher
    His Rose, Inc.
    Naperville, IL 60563-2534
    www.hisrose.org

Other books by His Rose, Inc.

    Johnny & His Rose: A True Story of Eternal Love

    The Legacy Campaign: Forty-Five Personal Accounts of Lives Forever Changed When Diagnosed with HIV/AIDS

    The First Twenty-Nine Days: Twenty True Stories of Re-Entry

    Secrets of a Survivor: Coming Out Smellin' Like a Rose

His Rose books are available at www.hisrose.org

Contact Abraham Rose at mysticalrose1940@gmail.com
Printed in the United States of America.

First Printing: 2011

To Johnny

*for his willingness to give God His way
and become the man God created him to be*

CONTENTS

Introduction
A Letter to You from Johnny
page vii

Preface
A Letter to You from Abraham Rose
page ix

Life Changing Love Letters to a Prisoner
October 1999 to December 2001
page 1

Addendum
Johnny's story of Re-Entry
page 99

Postscript
Johnny and Abraham Rose Today
page 105

INTRODUCTION

Dear Reader,

We are all prisoners, whether behind bars or not. Before these letters were written, I was a broken and empty man trying to fill a void that seemed like it had no bottom. I was distressed and in pain in my body, mind, and soul. It seemed as though the drugs and other substances had moved in and edged out my spirit.

These letters are proof that the Lord heard my cry. Yes, everything within me was crying out for help.

I remembered this Scripture in Psalm 50:15. It says Call upon me in the day of trouble. I will deliver you and you shall glorify Me. I knew that I needed deliverance from a power greater than myself. The drugs and other substances that I was using were taking me down a pathway that led to jails and institutions. The next step would surely be death.

First John 1:9 says, Confess your sins for He is faithful and just to forgive us our sins and cleanse us from all unrighteousness. My confession is "I was not arrested. I was rescued!" From that point on, I committed myself to the Lord. He took away the taste for cigarettes, alcohol, the desire to cuss, and the need to feel a part of persons, places and things that kept me in the darkness. I began to surround myself with positive, like-minded people.

Then I began to receive the letters. I got mail more frequently than most people I knew. The letters were filled with love and encouragement. I was able to share that love and devotion with some of my fellow inmates vicariously. The power in these letters was so potent it manifested itself in my demeanor and my conversation.

In prison, mail call is a sacred time. Everyone is expecting something, but many are disappointed when there is no mark by their name on the mail list. I was blessed to have a mark by my name a great deal of the time.

I pray that this book, "Dear John: Life Changing Letters to a Prisoner," blesses you and encourages you to write letters from your heart, honestly and sincerely. Good things will happen. The Lord will bless you and you will be a blessing to others.

Sincerely,
Johnny

PREFACE

August 17, 2006

Dear Friends,

There is no greater privilege than to love another human being and lead him to God. After the end of a painful twenty-five year marriage, I asked God if there was a man in the world for me. His answer was a resounding *No! But....there is one to whom I will lead you. You are to love him and lead him to Me.*

From our meeting in November of 1990 until I heard the words, "Well done, my good and faithful servant," Johnny became the center of my life.

After he backslid in 1998 God told me to take my hands off him. He almost killed himself in his insanity. He entered prison in September of 1999. By the power of the Holy Spirit, I loved him and ministered to him through these letters. When he was released in February of 2004, he was truly a new man, a new creation in Christ.

Johnny and I have decided to share these letters with you. May your spirit be nourished by this spiritual food. Like taking good medicine, by reading the "Dear John" letters, may you also blossom and grow. May you discover just who God created you to be. May you know the joy of finding your true purpose.

Yes, *the Truth makes you free!*
In God's love,
Abraham Rose

DEAR JOHN

Life Changing Love Letters to a Prisoner

Johnny Ellis #374452

OCTOBER, 1999

October 9, 1999

Dear John,

I woke up very early this morning with a heart full of passionate love for you. So I consciously sent it all to you via the Holy Spirit. I saw the Blood of Jesus being poured over you and filling you with His Divine Blood. Yes, you are healed. The Word says so!

I just reread your letter of 10-5-99, and I looked up your Bible references of 10-3-99. Yes, you were dead, but you are now alive again; you were lost, but now you are found. Because you believe in Him, *YOU SHALL NOT PERISH, BUT HAVE EVERLASTING LIFE* together with *your virtuous wife in whose heart you can safely trust.*

Do you see how God is blessing us? We are both alive again, alive to Love, the source of all life. This is a good example of: If you keep your mind on yourself, you will be depressed. If you keep your mind on your circumstances, you will be distressed. If you keep your mind on Christ, you will be at rest, and you will be your best!

You mentioned being a little in the dumps. I had the same experience. But reading, hearing, and meditating on the Word brought me out of it, and I am again filled to overflowing with life-giving JOY! My faith grows stronger each day. God has so much for us to accomplish through Christ who strengthens us. Now that we have rediscovered the love that God put in us for each other, nothing can stop us, ever.

John, you said you have nothing to do but pray and talk to God. In Proverbs 4:20-22 it says to keep your ears, eyes and heart focused on His Word, for they are life and health! Did you know that there are at least 32,000 blessings in the Bible? Let's find and claim them all. We'll never run out of things to do, and we'll never be bored. Remember, our lives are designed to bring us glory after glory. I too want to tell our story and share all the glory with you.

I thank and praise God that you are on His path, His path to life, love, and glory. That's the way we can go together. Thank you for choosing it. I always wanted to be with you.

Johnny Ellis #374452

October 18, 1999

Dear John,

John, have you read in detail the acts of Elisha? I have begun to read about him, and it is amazing. But, in particular, I'm reading 2 Kings 4:8-37 regarding the Shunammite woman. Boy, what a faith!!

She's the one who invited the Prophet to eat some food whenever he went to Shunem. Since he made a regular visit to Shunem, she and her husband made a small upper room with a bed, table, chair and a lamp stand so he would have a place to stay. She was rewarded with a son, but after several years, the boy died.

John, she put the little body onto the Prophet's bed, shut the door, and headed for the Prophet. When her husband asked why she was going to the Prophet, she said in 2 Kings 4:23, **IT IS WELL**.

When Elisha's servant came to greet her, and asked if it was well with her, she answered him **IT IS WELL**. And yet we see in verse 27 that *her soul is in deep distress...*

Of course Elisha restored her son to life. What a lesson! What a faith! What a motto! I'm adopting it. From now on, no matter what happens, I'm saying, as did the Shunammite woman, **IT IS WELL!**

John, the Bible is an amazing Book. It is the living Word. The more of the Word we get into our bellies, the more alive we become. I went to Sister V. for prayer yesterday, and she said to me, "Every time I see you, you look younger!" Someone else told me that I was glowing. John, I am a happy woman. God has made me marvelous promises that include you. So, no matter what happens, IT IS WELL! God's Will never fails. We can delay it all we want, which is all that has been happening. As soon as we make up our minds that we truly want what God wants, it's ours.

So stay in the Word, stay happy, and stay my husband. Continue to let me be the only woman you think about. Know that it was Divine Love that brought me to you. Know that God continues to pour out a torrent of Divine Love to you through me. Yes, it is not little me, but Love itself that loves you through me. And always remember with me that IT IS WELL.

Johnny Ellis #374452

October 24, 1999

Dear John,
    John, I know my husband is in there. The old man must die for us to ever have a real love and marriage. I am very happy now for two reasons. Number one, I know you are in a safe place. God is preserving you. Number two, I am free of the illusion that I have a husband when your first love is getting high. That's why you're in there! Don't even try to fool me this time, John. Your history shows me that, no matter what you said or did while locked up, the minute you came out, your main desire was not for God or me, but to return to your old life. When you do get out, I don't know what you'll do. But God knows your heart. He knows if you just want me around, but plan to continue in your old ways. So, I'm going to trust God all the way on this one. Only the Lord can cleanse you, and prepare you for His plan for your life. I believe that when you fully submit, I will know it.
    You must become a whole person, with Christ fully alive in you, directing your every breath, your every thought being in submission to Him. John, I never fell in love with the drug addict. God showed me the beauty of your soul when I looked into your eyes. The man I love and married was there. You can choose to be that man, to manifest the perfection of God in all you do, or you can serve your time, just waiting to "return to the vomit." Every time you use a curse word, every time you glorify your old life, you are going in the opposite direction of God's plan for us. I do love you, John. But it's time for you to grow up. It's time for you to put away your childish things and be the man that God created you to be. Then you will be ready to join me for a life of pure joy.
    Yes, John. I am a happy woman. Seek first the kingdom of God and His righteousness, and He will give you every wonderful thing, including me. I belong totally to God.
    'Bye for now.

Hi!
    You know there is only one possible ending to our story. Your deliverance, and the light of God shining on us as a couple, showing off the power of Love. Nothing else would make any sense.

Johnny Ellis #374452

So keep working on the manuscript. God is still God, and I still have my faith. Let's make this the greatest love story ever told!

October 28, 1999

Dear, Sweet Husband,
Do you fully realize what God was demonstrating yesterday regarding my visit? As it dawns on me, I marvel at His greatness. He wants us to know that no human power or law can touch His Holy Will.

When I awoke yesterday, I had my afternoon and evening planned, to see S. and A., and to go to Living Word. But, as always, I offered the entire day to the Lord. In this way, I submitted to His will, which He could then reveal to me. (If I had insisted on keeping my own plans, He would not have interfered.)

So, prompted by the Holy Spirit, I called Dodge Correctional to see if I could get a three hour visit yet, and found out I could, and the earliest I could come was 3:00 p.m. Then the thought and feeling came that "I **must** see you today," and to be ready to go by 10:00 a.m. This meant canceling my previous plans, which I did gladly. The thought of seeing you easily replaced everything else.

I arrived at Dodge at 3:10 p.m. and was processed by 3:45 p.m. Unbeknownst to me, ten minutes later Lobby received a notice to remove me from the visiting list. If I had arrived a little later, they would not have let me in! (The Lord knew all of this, and because of my obedience, was able to direct me so I could get to see you in spite of the will of other humans!)

The woman at the Lobby desk called Lt. R. and told him that I was already inside for the visit. He came to the visiting room for one reason...to evict me. But, again, our Lord was in charge. Unbeknownst to us, we found favor in his sight, and he overrode the order with the decision to let the visit continue. I learned this as I was leaving.

Shortly before the visit, you received notice that I had been removed from the visiting list. In order to demonstrate His supreme authority, the Lord then caused the visit to happen so that you could plainly see Who is in charge.

From this we learn not to trust what we see, hear, or feel, not to trust circumstances, but to totally trust our Lord. Only then

Johnny Ellis #374452

can He do miracles for us.

Now let's apply this lesson to your situation. No matter what you hear about your future, know that your life is in His hands if you are willing to stop listening to humans and begin to focus 100% on the Lord. He will direct your thoughts. He will direct your steps. He will lead you to the fulfillment of His perfect plan in your life. Circumstances are nothing to the Lord. He has all power, and He wants you to have it too. All He needs is your undivided attention. So, 23 hours a day in a cell is the perfect environment for you to practice God consciousness! Use this time wisely. Our future depends on it.

And please remember, *the joy of the Lord is our strength.* (Nehemiah 8:10) Joy is medicine, and you need a healthy dose of it. Seek the joy of the Lord. Your attention to this is essential to release God's power into your life...not just a little, but completely.

John, remember, this is an inside job. I just now tuned in to Pastor Winston on the radio, and he said, "If the inmates at Cook County jail correct their image, they will be out by next Wednesday!" What a confirmation of what I have been writing here to you!

Remember, *with God all things are possible.* Read Acts 16:19-26. In verses 25-26 we read, *at midnight Paul and Silas were praying and singing hymns to God, and the prisoners were listening to them. Suddenly there was a great earthquake, so that the foundations of the prison were shaken; and immediately all the doors were opened and everyone's chains were loosed.*

So John, please make up your mind that you want God's will, and God's will only, at work in your life. He will strengthen you, deliver you, and prepare you to do the impossible in this earth. You are very bright. As these truths sink into your very being, you will blossom according to God's will for you and nothing on this earth will have any power over you. This is my prayer for you, but only you can decide to do it.

Begin by putting all of your concerns into the Lord's hands. Every time a worry, fear, or concern pops into your mind, see the Lord's outstretched hands, and put that thought into His hands. He will take care of every detail of your life when you do this. And you may rest in perfect peace in His arms. Receive His divine love. You will then have more to give to others, including me!

John, no one loves you like God loves you, but no one in

Johnny Ellis #374452

the whole world loves you like I do. My love and my words are God's gift to you. Cherish them. Use them. Let my words nourish your spirit. As you learn and grow, your very presence will bless others.
    Remember, God is fully in charge when we let Him be. Seek His will continually. He will never leave you, and He will never let you down. Remember all the times He has already saved you. He is standing by, just waiting for you to acknowledge Him so He can take full charge of your life and lead you to the glory He has in store for you. Obey Him every moment. Let Him give you the words for the manuscript. It will flow perfectly from your pen, and I will do my part. *Eye has not seen, and ear has not heard, nor have entered into the heart of man the things which God has prepared for those who love Him.* (1 Corinthians 2:9)
    John, savor every moment there in that cell with Him. Enjoy this time. It will never come again. Stand back, and watch His glory!

Friday, October 29, 1999

To my Sweetheart,
    No more "Dear John." You are the man promised to me by God, so let's get it right this time. No more negatives from me! I have learned the power of confession!! *We know that all things work together for good for those who love God, to those who are the called according to His purpose.* (Romans 8:28) I'm tuning in with all my heart, soul, mind, and strength, sending unlimited love to you in every way the Spirit shows me. I know you're doing the same. Feel my presence morning, noon, and night. Seek God's will twenty-four hours a day. Let the Holy Spirit guide you every moment. John, there is no other way. We must go forward on the path He has made for us.
    See every temptation as an opportunity to strengthen your spirit, and your will. Remember, "I will to will Thy Will." And don't forget, "O. O. O." Your Open-mindedness to the Spirit of God turns every Obstacle to an Opportunity."
    So, my dear Mr. Author, how is the manuscript coming? Are you focusing on your eye view of everything? Oh, Honey, I just know that God has miracles waiting for us to claim them. But we must be faithful in small ways before He gives us the big stuff. So

Johnny Ellis #374452

continue to resist temptation, and be a light there in the darkness. Remember, Roszettae told us about "sending up timber." Well, you have time to build a real palace for us. So claim all of God's blessings. Call those things which are not yet as though they are. We both know that THEY WILL BE sooner than we can imagine.

God loves you, Honey, and so do I! You are still the most wonderful human being on the face of the earth, and that will never change. Right now, I may well be the only one who knows it, but someday we'll tell the world.

Johnny Ellis #374452

Johnny Ellis #374452

NOVEMBER, 1999

November 5, 1999

Hi Sweetie!
    John, my words to you are Life. Read my letters over every day, along with the Bible. You are in the perfect position to receive the nourishing Truth that will strengthen you for God's plan in your life.
    Never forget that where you are is a temporary condition, but also an important opportunity for you to purify and prepare yourself for the life God has for you. You must submit to the Lord with every thought you think, every breath you take, every beat of your heart. You know how easy it is to form a habit. When loving God becomes a habit, it is the easiest thing to do, and it manifests in all you do, shining your light into all the world.
    How is the manuscript coming? I hope I didn't discourage you. The first installment was absolutely brilliant. I just wanted to keep you on the right path. Sweetheart, I love you. Keep writing. It is our main source of communication right now.

November 8, 1999

Hello, Husband!
    It's Monday evening, and I just got your letter of November 4th today. At Living Word over the weekend I heard a preacher say that it does no good to ask God to take away a desire. He is a God Who fulfills our desires. So if you want to change your desires, you must will to do it yourself. I had a vivid dream about us this morning. In the dream you and I were going along a very narrow indented path of ice and snow. There was a rather large Caucasian woman guiding and helping us from behind. Not far away I could see another path alongside the one we were on, but flatter and wider. As soon as we got to the end of the path, you decided you needed something, and left. My heart was crying out, "Please, John, please don't. Not again!" But nothing would stop you. The next thing I knew, you were going back on the wider path. Perhaps my dream was telling me that it would do no good to help you now, because you still have the same old desires.
    But God is a good God, and He knows the desire of my

Johnny Ellis #374452

heart: to have the husband that He created for me. Only you can make him available to me by changing your desire. It's time for something brand new, John. It's an inside job. And only you can accomplish it. I will give you all the tools the Spirit of God tells me to.

I met "George" the other morning. He asked me for some money. I asked him if he knew where "Johnny" was. He indicated that "Johnny" used the needle, and wondered out loud if maybe "he" was dead. I didn't remind him that I was your wife. I hope he is right. I hope that the man who used those needles, and whatever else, is dead. Only then can the NEW MAN, the man created by God Almighty live in that body. It's up to you.

John, you're not going anywhere until you change on the inside. Then *ALL POWER IN HEAVEN AND ON EARTH* will rush in to deliver you. You know that I am obedient to the Spirit. I will drop everything and go to the President of the United States if need be when the Spirit of God let's me know you are ready. It's totally up to you. Remember, every curse word, every puff of a cigarette, keeping the company of low-life people, every negative thought, etc., all these things will retard your progress and keep you heading towards death. Choose life! Put no limits on what you are willing to do to be on the Godly path. Ask God, "Who am I? Where did I come from? Why am I here? What is my true purpose?" God will answer. Open your mind...O.O.O.!!! Seize this opportunity to be all that you are. Don't even try to fool us (God and me) again. I love my husband.

November 9, 1999

Hi Sweetie!

Who are you? A dope fiend bent on self destruction? Or the righteousness of God? Take your pick. You must choose again. You must consciously change your self image. If you don't, you will continue throwing away all of God's blessings. Do you understand me, John? It's nine years that we've been together. You should know better by now. I am still amazed at how you chose to live on the streets with people like George after I stood by you this past year through Mendota, Dane County Jail, Haymarket House, STD, abuse, watching you try to kill yourself. You really haven't given me any reason to believe that you wouldn't go right back to that if given

Johnny Ellis #374452

the opportunity.

If you are to be my partner, you must go all the way with God. You may not hold back one little thought or desire for the things of your past. You must change your mind about what you want. Stand up straight! Pull yourself out of the vomit. Only you can do it. Then the Lord will wash you clean with His blood. God won't interfere if you continue to think you can get away with your self abuse. You should know by now that you can't serve two masters. It's God or death. There's no other choice.

John, some months ago God told me clearly to take my hands off of you. Our relationship was literally killing me. My life was hell as was yours. The only difference is that I knew it. You acted like you were doing what you wanted to do. And you were.

No matter how much I love you, you are not going to fool me again. Right now it's a good thing that I can't see you or receive collect calls from you. I need to focus on my life, my ministry. I need to get on my feet financially.

I mentioned to someone that my husband and I aren't together right now. And the Lord spoke to me very clearly saying, "What do you mean? You know that I am with you always. Did you forget that I AM your Bridegroom, your True Love, your Husband? Did you forget your promise to Me, to be My wife and serve Me all of your life, which is eternity?"

So you see, John, I have my own things to remember. God is working on both of us, perfecting us for His perfect plan. He needs His temple to be in good repair so He can join me here on earth. So just invite Him in. You just don't know what you've been missing by excluding Him. Let Him live in you. Let Him love through you. Let me love you. Let me love God in you. Can you just imagine how it will be?!

Friday, November 12, 1999

Sweetheart!

My passion and desire is mounting as I think about your book, our book. We must set a definite goal, have a clear vision of what this book will accomplish on the highest level. Seeking first God's kingdom, all else, freedom, prosperity, opportunity for world travel, etc. will surely follow.

So help me with this, John. Let's seek God's will together,

Johnny Ellis #374452

so that we can clearly share this vision. Get back to your writing. Be uninhibited, as you started out. God will guide your writing and the editing. I need your raw material to build on. You know you are a genius. Let your light shine in the pages. The world will be delighted.

Honey, I don't remember when I've ever been so excited about a project...probably never. This is it. This is our ticket. So write, write, write! God will give the increase. He will do exceedingly, abundantly above anything we could ask or think. Sweetheart, I am so happy and confident in our love. Your manuscript makes me giggle every time I read it. You are so beautiful. I love you so much. There will never be another man for me. You are the one He promised. I claim that promise now, in the glorious name of Jesus! Nothing can hold back the power of love. Nothing can stop us now. We have all the power of the universe behind us, the power of Divine Love.

Sunday, November 14, 1999

My Love, I just opened my Bible to Song of Solomon. In Chapter 3, verse 2, *I will rise now, I said, And go about the city; in the streets and in the squares I will seek the one I love.* (That's how I found you, Sweetheart!) Verse 12, *A garden enclosed is my sister, my spouse,* v. 16, *Let my beloved come to his garden and eat its pleasant fruits.*

Chapter 5, v. 11-12, *His locks are wavy, and black as a raven. His eyes are like doves.* (That's how I see you, Honey.) And in Chapter 6, she is referred to as *"O fairest among women,"* called *"blessed."* Chapter 2:3, *I sat down in his shade with great delight, and his fruit was sweet to my taste,* and v. 16, My *beloved is mine and I am his,* chapter 8:6, *Set me as a seal upon your heart, as a seal upon your arm.*

God is showing me that our story will rival Solomon's Song as you tell the world of God's love for us, and our love for each other. You will show His hand in our lives every step of the way so that there will be no doubt in the reader's mind Who is in charge. So write, John, write your ticket to freedom, your passport to heaven on earth. Write your check for the abundance and prosperity God has in store for you. It is all already yours. God has

Johnny Ellis #374452

given you every thing you need to claim it. Write, write, write! You know I will do my part, that you will have a perfect book to present to the world.

Sweetheart, for now, put aside all other wishes and desires, and concentrate, be single minded about your manuscript. Always pray and seek the Holy Spirit's guidance as you write. You are a masterpiece. Let your essence flow onto the page. Let your glory rise up in print. You are my beloved. I want the world to know.

Saturday morning, November 20, 1999

Hi Sweetie!

Come and have breakfast with me. There are potatoes baking in the oven. And in the large frying pan, with a little olive and canola oil are sliced red onion, split baby carrots, and the white and green flowers of cauliflower and broccoli. When all is cooked, I will peel and slice the potatoes and add them to the pan, along with pieces of tofu. Then I will season and spice it to taste. Won't you join me? I made enough for you too.

Imagination is a wonderful thing. I can see you, here and now, with me, forever in this moment. I can feel your closeness, your breath on my neck. Now I hear your sweet voice, saying my name, moaning softly. Life is good! Life is ONE. We are one. Never separate. Only our thoughts can lead to the belief in separation. In truth. there is no such thing.

So, it is easy to see how two people could physically be in the same location, but experience being alone and lonely, separation. That's what happened to us, Honey. This past year, even when we were in the same apartment, the same room, the same bed, our hearts and minds were not together. Now, though miles apart, we are one in love, our hearts and souls sing one melody, you are mine and I am yours. I pray to the Lord to show us how to let it always be this way; that we may delight in each other's physical presence and not lose the spiritual connection, not stray into other paths.

Johnny Ellis #374452

Monday morning, November 22, 1999

My Sweet Husband,

Yesterday, at church, I felt your presence. You were physically with me, and I could feel my arms around your slim waist. And then it got even more erotic...right there during the Praise and Worship Service! I'm feeling your "being" close to me more and more. Your love for me must be growing stronger. Praise God! Thank you, Lord!

As we trust the Spirit of God, doors will open, opportunities will arise, and miracles will manifest. As I grow happier, younger and healthier each day, my heart is in constant communion with the Lord. When I consider the future, you are always there, by my side. I cannot even imagine life without you.

God has given us the gift of life, with free will. Only when we give that life back to God in total surrender can we begin to realize the fullness of life. That is the only true purpose of "free will." It's not God's will for us to abuse our minds and bodies unto death, but we can learn from these things the difference between the path to death and the path to life. Then we can choose again, choose "life." Once we have made the choice of life, the Holy Spirit empowers us, the Good Shepherd leads and guides us, and God Himself smiles on us. So I thank God that you have finally chosen "LIFE" because God is Life, God is Love, and we can only be together in God, in Life, and in Love. It is all the same.

A few months ago I never could have kept up this pace. But with the joy comes new energy. Yes, I am constantly renewed by my beloved God. I am tapped into the highest. He sustains me abundantly. Since we are one, John, this same power flows into you. Practice being conscious of it morning, noon and night. The more we think about it, the stronger it becomes. So just consider God, Life, Love, and your Rose constantly. You can't go wrong. You've got it made.

Create a scenario in your mind of us together again...waking up in the morning in each other's arms...enjoying a leisurely breakfast together, praying together, planning our day guided by the Holy Spirit, with no interference from anyone or anything...just you, me and God. Tell me about it. I love you, Sweetie.

Johnny Ellis #374452

Friday, November 26, 1999

Hi Honey!
    I still believe that this is an inside job. Are you smoking, cursing, desiring what is less than loving for yourself? Or are you sincerely giving the Lord all your love, all your attention, all your devotion? Only you know the answer. But one thing I do know, if you are making the Lord your all, praying without ceasing, there will be fruit. No one can make this choice for you. Choose God. Choose Life. Choose Love. Choose Freedom to live and love God. Then all else will be added to this.
    John, there's so much more to our lives than our "past." In your days in that cell, ask God to reveal to you the journey of your soul. God can take you to amazing places, no matter that your body is locked up. You can visit yourself from the beginning of time, in many lives and situations. God will guide you on this journey within. Ask for this experience. Your life will be greatly enriched as you experience the beauty of your soul.
    I received your latest manuscript installment. You are definitely on the right track. This is something that will inspire others. Continue to find the very best within yourself. No matter what the computer says, you are my beautiful, wonderful husband!

Sweet Lord, Jesus Christ. I look to you for direction. I trust you completely. This marriage has been new territory for me from the beginning. Only you know the way. This life of mine I have given to you. Only You can lead me and guide me out of the darkness of sickness and poverty into Your light of health and prosperity. Only You can lead my husband out of the prison of his mind and body to the light of freedom.

November 30, 1999

Hi, Sweetie!
    Remember, Honey, seek ye first the kingdom of God and His righteousness, then all these things will be added to it. Keep your heart, soul, mind and strength focused on the goodness of the Lord, and all of your good, pure, and wonderful thoughts will come to pass.

Johnny Ellis #374452

Johnny Ellis #374452

DECEMBER, 1999

Wednesday, December 1, 1999

Good Morning, Love,
　　Today I awoke with a fresh perspective. We are living in faith, Honey. But I'm ready for the fruit, the manifestation of more than fifteen years of total surrender to God. Can you imagine how great it will be as it begins to materialize. So you just keep training your mind, heart, soul and spirit to stay on the path. The order is (1) Thought, (2) Word, (3) Deed. It all begins with a thought. Some of the thoughts come from the subconscious, placed there in your childhood without you knowing it, a lie that you accepted as a truth, the belief in self abuse as "good." You need to go back into your childhood, and remember where you got that idea, that thought, and take another look at it. And then, in the light of what you now know, create a new thought, a thought that includes the highest good that you can imagine, a life of love and peace and goodness. I love you, Sweetie.

God, again I surrender. I can of mine own self do nothing, but I can do all things through Christ Who strengthens me. But what shall I do?

Thursday night, December 2, 1999

Hi, Honey!
　　How I wish you hadn't decided to go back to drugs. You never would have hurt another human being in your right mind. You wouldn't have had to go back to jail. How I wish you had chosen to stay clean and sober, and to be a husband to me. I really enjoyed being with you when you were clean and sober. Why did you do it? At least you have all of your needs taken care of. And you are being protected from yourself. You must have known that you were killing yourself. You are not a stupid man. Why were you doing it?
　　You need to answer these questions, if not for me, at least for yourself. If you don't clear this up in your mind, you will continue doing the same thing until you die.

Johnny Ellis #374452

It's Friday morning, December 3, 1999.

Good Morning, My Husband!

If you entertain the slightest thought that when we're together again that you can still do your "stupid shit," you must change your mind, which is the meaning of the word "repent," to rethink your beliefs. John, I'm serious about this. We don't have time for your nonsense, and that's exactly what it is...no sense! You have been gifted with a brilliant mind, and an outstanding character. Thank God for these beautiful qualities. Ask forgiveness for abusing the gifts that God gave you...not just your mind and character, but your wife too.

Do you understand what you are doing when you defile yourself even with thoughts of that old life, or with curse words coming out of your mouth? Remember your graduation speech, how you blessed hundreds of people with your words. Thank God for this gift, and it is truly a gift. John, don't let one word unworthy of the Christ in you pass from your loving lips.

In a previous letter I began to speak of (1) Thought, (2) Word, and (3) Deed. When a less-than-loving word comes forth from your mouth, you must immediately go back to the thought from where it came, and change that thought. Remember that we create with our words, so the next thing that happens is that you do exactly what you think and say, or you manifest it in your life. The Bible says we should only think on what is good and lovely and pure.

You must purify your mind if you sincerely want to be my husband. Anything less will destroy you. Begin to visualize exactly what you will do when you get out. See yourself in situations thinking pure thoughts, saying loving words, and creating a beautiful, Godly life. You can do all this there in that cell. What better place to change your life. In the past you came out doing exactly the same thing you did to get in. This time it must be different. This is probably your last chance. Choose life or death, blessing or curse. As for me and my household, I choose to live and glorify God in all ways, always.

Be the man that God created you to be. Be that man right now right where you are. Nothing can stop the soul's journey back to the Father. Go all the way. Don't let anyone or anything stop you. Time means nothing. It's what you do with each moment that

Johnny Ellis #374452

counts. Purify your life. God is with you, and I will be there to receive my husband.

Saturday, December 4, 1999

Hi Honey!
    John, I love you, and I love your letters. I especially love the prayers you put at the beginning of the letters. Keep writing your book. I know the inspiration will come for me to edit it all. I loved your story about your "gang." I don't remember hearing about all those dogs.
    It's hard to believe that so many years have already passed since we met. Signs and wonders, that's what I'm ready for. Signs and wonders. I'll keep praying, and keep my faith. We both have to reach inside and connect with the Source of all love, power, and strength. The final chorus of the "Messiah" was taken from Revelation 5:12. "Worthy is the Lamb that was slain, and hath redeemed us to God by His blood, to receive power, and riches, and wisdom, and strength, and glory and blessing." I wish all of these good things for you.

Monday, December 6, 1999

Good Morning, dear Husband,
    Yesterday morning I awoke in your arms in the middle of a deep passionate kiss. And this morning I could feel you inside me. So, it looks like YOU are my spirit lover. I suspect it was you all along. John, there's so much more to us than we can imagine. As you awaken to your Spirit, you begin to grasp the power potential that you have. I know I'm not imagining things. I feel your presence, I feel your love and your warmth.
    You mentioned "osteoporosis" in your last letter. Did you know that exercise builds up the bone mass? Just holding up your arms and hands when you pray will strengthen you. You can always do a few push ups, etc. Are you doing anything for your physical fitness? If not, begin, and always be mindful of the Lord as you do.
    This morning I saw a man across the street from me and, from a distance, he looked just like you. I couldn't help staring at him. He turned his head towards me, and I swear, I saw your face.

Johnny Ellis #374452

I got into the car, and tears started streaming down my face. And as I write these words, the tears are coming again. I miss you more than I realized. John, our spiritual connection is growing stronger. Remember, whatever we manifest in the spirit will come to be! We will be together again, maybe sooner than we can know.

Go for it, Honey. Reach out and claim what is yours. Claim your wife, claim your life! Claim the kingdom of God on earth. Claim your power in the universe. Claim it all, John. It's already yours. God has given it all. Just reach out and take it. Be single minded. Stay on the path. Whatever else comes into your mind, just put it in the Lord's hands. He knows what to do with it. I'm ready for you. I'm ready for my husband. I'm ready for the life that God promised us!

Keep the love coming, Sweetie. I am receiving it and it fills me with wonder and joy. I love you. Love heals all things, cures all things. Love is all there is. You are my love, my all.

Tuesday night, December 7, 1999

Oh, My Poor Dear Sweet Husband,

God sent me to you to extricate you from the world, not to sink you deeper into the darkness! How can you even think of asking me for a television set? I was so amazed as I read your letter postmarked December 2nd, which I received today. You are still looking to the world to occupy your mind.

Did you forget, *Seek FIRST the kingdom of God and His righteousness, THEN all these things will be added to you.* Have you not yet discovered that there is a world beyond the ignorance you see around you? Just because the others waste their God-given minds on the nonsense that comes through the TV screen, you think you must do the same. Think, John, think! Might God have another purpose for your eyes and ears than gluing them to the boob-tube?

Just ASK Him. A.S.K. Ask, Seek, and Knock. *Ask and you will receive. Seek and you will find. Knock and it will open to you.* In the world *there is a way that seems right to man, but the end of which is death.* Raise your vision to God. Ask Him what you should seek, what door you should knock on. Tap into your God-given intelligence. God will give you something wonderful to do with your time if you let Him. Be like Joseph. He spent many years

Johnny Ellis #374452

in prison, but he was always a leader. Rise up, John! Rise above your surroundings. Don't sink to the level of the masses. Dare to be different. Dare to be God's man. Dare to stand up straight. Dare to let the joy of the Lord be your strength. Dare to be the man God created you to be. Dare to be my Husband.

My Sweet Darling, I see so much more to you than meets the eye. You must get to know yourself. You must get past your beliefs that you acquired in the world and find the truth that God put in you. Dig, John, dig! Don't keep filling your mind with garbage. Dump it all out, and discover the beautiful, creative mind God gave you, the mind created to have dominion over all the earth. Once you find yourself, television will hold no attraction for you. Nor will drugs, alcohol, or filth of any kind.

John, you may reject my words, but in doing so, you reject me, and the One who sent me to you. I tell you the truth. I don't know if anyone else has ever told you the truth. I do know that you have believed many lies about yourself, and the family that you knew as you grew up had only negative expectations of you. When we got together, they were amazed at the man you became. But then you threw it all away. God is giving you another chance. Take it or leave it. It's all up to you. If you want the ignorance and filth of the world, it will be without me. I have made my choice, and I'm going all the way with God.

I will continue sending love to you. I will continue praying for you. But you are making your own choice. The world has lied to you, John, and you keep choosing to believe it. Take a look at yourself. Take a look at your surroundings. This is your choice. You have created your life just as it is. Into your life God has sent me to reach out my hand to you. I have done so. But I suspect that you have only seen me as a means to get what you thought you wanted and needed, what the world told you was important. Think again, John, yes, repent, re-think...before it's too late.

Monday, December 13, 1999

Hi Sweetie!

Thank you for the additional manuscript. Keep working on the perfect ending to the story, the emergence of God's perfected man, and my true husband. Think of yourself as a caterpillar, and the prison as a cocoon. When you emerge you will be a beautiful

Johnny Ellis #374452

butterfly who will glorify God. You are being transformed every moment. Remember to go for the T.O.P., Trust, Obedience, and Patience. You can't miss!

Wednesday, December 15, 1999

Hi, My Sweet, Darling Husband!
　　　John, loving God is a great adventure. To know Him is to love Him. The more we know Him and love Him and surrender to Him, the more He reveals His goodness and great glory in our lives.
　　　John, I just looked up John 15:7-8, which you wrote in your letter of 12-8-99. How perfectly in harmony it is with my writing yesterday and today. *If you abide in Me, and My words abide in you, you will ask what you desire, and it shall be done for you. By this My Father is glorified, that you bear much fruit, so you will be My disciples.* We do abide in Him, and His words abide in us. So ask John, ASK! It shall be done for us. What a great God we serve! Self-discovery is the greatest adventure of all. I love you

Wednesday, December 22, 1999

My Precious Husband,
　　　God is so good. I believe, Honey. I have faith that our confession is now and forever true. Nothing can ever again keep us apart. Remember, once we are bound together in Spirit, the rest will naturally fall in place. Even though we cannot be physically together I do feel closer to you than ever. We are partners, on the same team.
　　　Yes, I will type the manuscript...after the Holidays. John, if I type it as is, with all the loving left in, will you be sharing it with others? Or is it just for you. Let me know!
　　　I love you. I love your letters. I love your Scriptures. I love your love for me and God. I love your strength. I love your willingness to follow Spirit. I love that you are God's man. I love that you are my man! I love that God brought me to you. I love that we are one. I love that God is working in our lives in such a wonderful way to show His glory. I love that we are growing young and healthy, heart, soul, mind, and body. I love that God continually blesses us and leads us in the right path, according to

Johnny Ellis #374452

His Will.

December 12, 1999

Oh John!
 The Holy Spirit guides my fingers as I write these words. I just awoke holding your sweet face in my hands, thinking, telling you, how beautiful you are. Suddenly the horror hit me. You were going through the crucifixion! And I was there, seeing it all. It was you carrying the cross, bloody, in agony and pain. And I was right there, seeing, feeling it all with you.
 I have been seeing these images, you as Christ, more and more. But this morning, the full agony hit me, and I suffered with you. John, you are not alone. Our souls are one. Whatever you are going through, my soul feels it too. But don't be afraid. Look to God. He will deliver you.
 This is what our Lord demonstrated so clearly. When we are focused on the Lord, there is no death. And He arose glorified, with all power in heaven and on earth. Claim this, John, claim this for you and for me. Seize all that is yours, by the will of God Most High. He wants to exalt you, to lift you up to the glory He has in store for you. Believe. Receive. Don't look to the left or to the right. Fix your gaze upon God, from Whom comes your salvation.
 Be the Miracle God created you to be. Be all that you are. Blossom as the beautiful glorious flower made by God. There's a German Christmas song that describes Christ as a rose blooming in the winter snow. You are there, in the winter of that prison, without warmth, without sunshine, but with the grace of God, you are blossoming, you are coming forth triumphant. Nothing can stop your soul's journey back to the Father, our Source. Go all the way to oneness with the Creator. Only then will you experience your True Self. Don't be afraid, Honey. I'm with you. I have always been with you. I will never leave you. God put us together. I love you with a Love Divine.

 It's 5:30 a.m., Wednesday morning. I love you so much, Honey. You are so precious to me. I thank God for you. I know that we will be together again, together forever, for the purpose that God ordained. Just say "Yes, yes, Lord," say "yes" to all He desires for you. "Yes, yes, yes, yes, Lord, yes. Yes!" Your mind is

Johnny Ellis #374452

purified. You are free from all illusions, free to see and hear from the Lord, free to follow His will for you. Nothing can hold you back ever again! And nothing can keep me from you. Forget about the world, or what appears to be. I AM WITH YOU. NOTHING CAN KEEP ME FROM YOU. If you will, you can see me and feel me right here and now, right where you are. Our love transcends time and space, and I answer "yes" to your every desire.

Honey, God just gave me a vision. We are together, and I am comforting you. I see my heart, no longer inside, but, looking like the sacred heart of Christ, beating on the outside of my chest. It is a sacred and divine love I have for you. The love of God for you beats in my heart. He has made me a channel of His love for you. And I am obedient to His desires. I won't hold back.

Right now it seems that our letters are the main source of our communication, but there is much more, without having to go through the red-tape of the prison system. We are together. We are one. We can experience each other any time, any place. As we practice this holy oneness, with God and with each other, our togetherness becomes a reality, and **it will manifest** before we know it.

Be of good faith. Have courage. God is still in charge, and nothing happens without His full knowledge and control. Look to His goodness. Look to His love. Look to His mercy. Look to the fullness of His plan for your life. It is an inside job. I love you!

Christmas, 1999

Good Morning, Sweet Husband!
Happy Anniversary and Merry Christmas. John, I'd like to share with you a little prayer I wrote for us:
Dear Lord, We come to You this Christmas Day and give You our whole hearts. We come in faith, knowing that whatever we ask in Your name is already ours. And so we present with clarity to You our heart's desires. We trust that we experience the essence of all we seek, here and now, with our total devotion to You manifesting much fruit.

We have given You our lives in total surrender. We love You. We thank You. We praise You. We glorify You. Your great glory is manifest in our lives. Our light so shines before mankind that You are glorified in all the earth. Amen.

Johnny Ellis #374452

    Is there any doubt in your mind that we will have all of this and more? I believe, Honey, I believe! So prepare yourself. Each moment of your life, right now, live it with God, through the Christ within you. Let your light shine right there. Your body may be in prison, but your mind is free, free to unite with your Maker, to be one with your Source, free to be with me at will. Experience your oneness with God and with your spouse now each and every day, and it will certainly manifest at the right time. He promised, and God keeps His promises. You are the desire of my heart. I love you, Sweetie.

Johnny Ellis #374452

Johnny Ellis #374452

JANUARY, 2000

Wednesday evening, January 5, 2000

Hi, Sweetie! Happy New Millennium!
With the new Millennium, I believe that people are more conscious of spirituality than ever before, so I know that the day is coming when they will welcome my message of God's love.
John, your letters thrill me. I love the way you talk to God. Your "Love Confession" is very beautiful.
Dee, our massage lady, said she asked Jesus to show himself to her. Then she saw a man who looked just like you. You figure it out! I love you, Sweetie!

Friday morning, January 6, 2000

Hi, Angel,
It was wonderful hearing your voice last night. And what a great report of your health, and physical fitness. No, we're not meant to get old, sick, and decrepit. God's plan is for us to be young and vital eternally. We must get into harmony with God's plan. This is an inside job, and you are in the perfect position to do this work!
Father, we praise You and thank You that You are with John, in him, and all around him, that he may blossom to become all that you have created him to be. Continue to guide him on this inward journey to the fulfillment of Your plan for him. Amen.
John, we must break through your old thinking habits, to the fresh, new you underneath. The Holy Spirit has given me an idea. Each day reach for one of my letters, guided by the Holy Spirit. Read all or part of it, again letting the Holy Spirit guide you. Pray and meditate on it, and write the results, as in a journal. Perhaps once a week, mail your writings to me. (1) Read. (2) Meditate. (3) Write.
You need time to forget about circumstances and self, and begin to discover "Self," your Higher Self. This is the part of you that is truly my husband, the part that I am totally in love with, the part that God showed to me when I met you. It has nothing to do with how you lived, or what you said or did, because you were so out of harmony with your true Self. Now is the time for your

Johnny Ellis #374452

outward manifestation to perfectly line up with your true Higher Self. John, as you do this, you will discover your power in the universe to manifest God's perfection in all you do and say.

Sweetheart, why should I settle for less? Why should I sit back and let you continue as you have been all these years, traveling foolishly down the road leading to death. I found the video tape I made when you were "high" and trying to fill an ice cube tray. Great comedians have made a lot of money acting like they were drunk or high. This tape really makes me laugh. If for one moment I thought that this was really you, what a tragedy that would be. But, in my heart, I know the real you. So I can laugh at these "precious moments," my adorable husband acting the fool.

Sweetheart, my heart is so full of love for you, it's ready to explode. But now it must be tough love. God has been preparing your heart, soul, mind and strength for this next leg of your journey, your journey inward.

Begin each day with the prayer: *Holy Spirit, I give this day to You. Lead me, guide me to a fuller realization of who I am, who God, my Father and Creator intended for me to be. I submit to your guidance, because I desire with all my heart, soul, mind and strength to fully realize your plan for my life. In the name of our precious Lord and Savior, Jesus Christ, Amen.*

Again, Honey, why should I settle for less? God led me to you, my true husband, and I recognized you even though you were living an illusion. Now it's time for your real Self to shine through, my husband, partner, friend, lover, mate, my all.

Monday Morning, January 17, 2000

Good Morning, Sweetheart!

God loves you sooooo much. I'm sure you are hearing it directly from God. And you are also hearing it through me. Yes, God speaks to you through me. I am just the messenger, and I am obedient in bringing the message clearly by the power of the Holy Spirit. So open your spiritual eyes and ears, open your heart wide, and receive.

Are you ready for your miracle? Or are you expecting to rot in that cell? Believe. Receive. I heard a story about a town that was taken over by the enemy. All the young men were put into prison. One kind soul sold everything he had and bought pillows and blankets for all the men so they could be comfortable. A second kind soul offered all the produce from his farm so that the men could have enough to eat. A third kind soul bought television sets for all the men, so that their minds would be occupied and they wouldn't have to think of the fact that they were in prison. But then the spiritual master came. At night he stole the keys, and released all the prisoners.

Do you see, John, the comfort, food, and recreation just keep you there. Don't get comfortable! Continue to seek the Lord's face. Continue to cry out for complete freedom, not just freedom for your body, but freedom for your very heart, soul, and spirit. Don't settle for less than that.

Read Acts 12:3-19, where Peter is miraculously released from prison. This is an inside job, Honey. Get your heart, soul, mind and strength in harmony with God's will, and He will make a way where there is no way. The Lord also wants you to meditate on David. *David danced for joy before the Lord with all his might.* (2 Samuel 6:14) Now read 1 Samuel 22:12-15 and 23:1. *...he changed his behavior...* Begin your ministry right there in that cell. Sing and dance before the Lord with all your heart and soul. Your joy in loving the Lord is your strength. It will open doors!

John, I give you the key to total freedom. Read this letter over and over. Study it. Ask the Holy Spirit to enlighten your mind to its true meaning. Ask the Holy Spirit to reveal through these words the key to your freedom. With God all things are possible. He has already made a way for you. You must sincerely seek His way. Don't waste any more time wallowing in self pity. Come out of that place! Awaken to the glory of the Lord, which is fully present in that cell, just awaiting your attention, so you can be led and guided to the fulfillment of His plan in your life. I wait for you, my love.

Saturday Morning, January 29, 2000

My Precious Love,

Earlier this week I sent a hand written letter to you expressing my appreciation of who you are and all you are accomplishing there in that cell. As we journey within our very selves, we discover wealth untold. We discover unity with all of life, and a direct connection to Divine Mind, where we are all at

Johnny Ellis #374452

home. All else is illusion, ignorance, sin. We need no longer settle for less than Divine Perfection, which is our true nature.

Thank you, Sweetie, for your love and prayers that you are sending up on my behalf. God is working in a mighty way in my life. Next Thursday, in my ministry class, we are to speak five minutes on our "Vision Statement." This morning The Lord revealed to me that "the fullness of the Spiritual Mother dwells in me as the fullness of the Son dwelt in Jesus." Then I had a vision of mankind shouting out, "Mama's home!" and there was great rejoicing throughout the earth. As we remember who we are, we "come home" to the life God ordained for each of us.

As the Spiritual Mother I lead all of my children back home to the Father, where we dwell together forever in peace and harmony. Sounds like a big order, but I know that I can do all things through Christ which strengthens me. So I will not hold back, but step out in boldness just as dear Jesus did when he said, "If you have seen Me, you have seen the Father."

Where are you, John, on your spiritual journey? What revelation are you receiving of who you are and why you're here?

Write soon. I love you.

Johnny Ellis #374452

FEBRUARY, 2000

Saturday morning, February 12, 2000

Hi Sweetie!
    I have your letter before me postmarked February 7. Thank you for all your good thoughts, wishes and feelings about my move. Yes, it certainly is a step in the right direction. We are learning how to create our own lives, according to spiritual principles, "ask believing, and you will receive."
    Your letters seem to be growing in depth of beauty and love. Last night I had a wonderful dream. I was with a group of people, and I looked up and saw Jesus in a shimmering white graduation gown and mortarboard (the graduation cap). He was absolutely radiant, smiling and walking to the left, reaching out and receiving a diploma. This morning, in my meditation, I realized that "Jesus" looked just like you.
    I asked the Lord, and received an affirmative. But, I thought it was Jesus. Again I received an affirmative. Can you understand that?
    In a book called "Conversations with God, an uncommon dialogue," I quote, "If you do not go within, you go without. There is nothing you cannot be, do, or have." This is very much in keeping with the Bible's "Seek ye first the kingdom of God and His righteousness, and all these things will follow." Once you have found your way to oneness with God, having made that your single-minded goal, nothing else will matter. That's when you'll get your TV. You alone are responsible for your life.
    I love you, Honey. I thank you, God, that everything I do blesses my mate too! Be blessed, Sweetheart. Oh yes, and be my Valentine too. In the name of Jesus!

Tuesday, February 29, 2000

Dear John,
    Thank you for all of your recent letters. Yes, they are filled with love and passion. But it is clear that there is one thing on your mind underlying all else; your love for television. Joshua didn't have a TV. David didn't have a TV. Jesus didn't have a TV. They all loved God totally, and prayed without ceasing morning, noon, and night. In their lifetimes they reached oneness with God. If they

Johnny Ellis #374452

had had the distraction of television, they never, I repeat, NEVER could have blossomed into the men God created.

So, you still want a television, an idol to bow down before, day and night, Satan's tool to suck your brain out of your head. In the Great Commandment we are told to love God with all of our heart, soul, mind and strength. But you are willing to surrender your mind to television. I'm sorry that you don't want more for yourself. But obviously you don't know what it means to surrender totally to God, and discover your own true identity, created by the Almighty.

Right now you have the opportunity to give your whole self to God, and thereby to blossom into the work of His hand. You will find your true self only by going within. You are still looking out into the world to occupy your mind, and to waste your time and your life. You think you "need" a TV. because you still don't know the true purpose of life. I will continue to pray for your enlightenment. But, guess what? If and when you do get your TV, there's no way you will be able to continue to grow spiritually. Consequently there will be no hope for us as a couple. I will never settle for a man who seeks his fulfillment in the world.

Yes, John, God showed me the beauty of your soul when we met. That is the man I fell in love with. You are being given every opportunity to manifest that man in the flesh. If you continue to seek the pleasures of the world, and it doesn't matter if it's TV, drugs, illicit sex, or whatever, you are moving away from God rather than towards Him. As the Bible says, you can't serve two masters. If you choose God, I will be there. If you continue to seek the darkness and ignorance of the world, then there is nothing for me to hope for. Your mind will grow feeble, and your body will decay. If you don't change on the inside, when you come out of prison, you will just return to the vomit. And I want no part of that.

So, John, do you really still want a television set? Is this really the only life you can envision for yourself. Then I have failed. I wanted so much more for you. Again, I will continue to lift you in prayer as a fellow human being. But, as far as you ever being my partner in Christ, you are taking away my hope. Remember the prayer, "I will to will Thy will." Do you really believe God wants you to have a television? Try saying this prayer and see if it makes a difference in your will. For me to get you a television would be the same as getting a divorce. It would be the end of hope for us to be

Johnny Ellis #374452

together in the joy and harmony ordained by God. "And if it seems evil to you to serve the Lord, choose for yourself this day whom you will serve, whether the gods of sex, drugs, or television. But as for me and my house, we will serve the Lord." (Joshua 24:15)

If you still want a TV, you don't need to write to me again. God told me to take my hands off of you when you continued to stay in the streets. You still haven't learned what it means to give your whole self to God, and I won't settle for less. Like Jonah, you are in the belly of the whale. What more can God do to get your full attention?

Johnny Ellis #374452

Johnny Ellis #374452

MARCH, 2000

Wednesday, March 22, 2000

Hi Sweetie,

Last night, in a vision, I was surrounded by demons. They at first seemed to be in men's bodies, but then I realized the bodies were dead and putrid, the clothes hung on them, but the faces were alive with all the evil of Satan's demons, eyes all focused on me, ready to attack. Some were even wearing police uniforms. Suddenly one began to glide directly towards me. As it reached me, I heard the words, "Don't touch her!" And he glided right by me. I immediately lifted my eyes to heaven and started talking to God. I reminded Him of all the wonderful promises He had given me, including immortality, unceasing energy, and power to do His work. I soon was conscious only of God, and the power of my words to Him. I was surrounded with a beautiful light, and when I finally looked around me, there was no trace of the demons. VICTORY!

Yes, Honey, I believe God has prosperity for us, but it's more that "properity" as you spell it. It means much more than property, or material things. I reach out and claim abundance of love, joy, peace, health, happiness, strength, the light of God flowing through me, my oneness with God, etc. Without these things, materiality is meaningless. I'm ready for abundance of joy.

The spiritual path is an eternal path. Journey with me on this path so we can discover together all the gifts our Heavenly Father has for us. They are already ours. We must focus on God with whole heart, soul, mind and strength to find them.

Johnny Ellis #374452

Johnny Ellis #374452

APRIL, 2000

Tuesday, April 4, 2000

Hi Sweetheart,
The prayers of a righteous man avail much. Please thank all of the dear ones who have been praying for me. And my love and thanks especially to you. John, your prayers are powerful and much needed. I have been under attack. Each day I grow stronger and more joyful, and the swelling on my neck gets less and less. Today I awoke with a strange rash all over my body! I just had to laugh at the lengths Satan will go to try to get me down. But it won't work. He is a defeated foe. Our Lord knocked him out in the first round two thousand years ago. He's acting like he's still in the fight, but I refuse to give him any power.

Please keep those prayers coming, not just for complete healing, but for full power in the Name of Jesus to do, say, and be all that God created me to do, say, and be! Help me to launch "His Rose, Inc., a Ministry of Love, Truth and Beauty," that my light shall shine, illuminating the entire universe for God's glory. I prayed and prayed to be "all that I am," and I won't settle for less! Are you listening, God? Your Rose is stepping out, and claiming to be the Miracle you said I am.

My fingers are beginning to fly over the piano keys. I pray as I play for the Holy Spirit to use me. It is not I, but Christ in me Who does the work. I am a willing channel for God's Love to reach the earth, filling the hungry souls with spiritual food. So, partner, are you not in a perfect position to be my prayer warrior! And I am thrilled that you are calling others to join you in making your petitions known to God. Feel the power, John. Know that where two or more are gathered in His Name, He is there. And He has promised to give us anything we ask in His Holy Name. So tell Him about "His Rose." Tell Him about "your Rose," whom He sent to you to lead you out of the darkness. Tell Him if I'm doing a good job! Tell Him about my love. Tell Him to send His angels to accompany me as I step out for His glory, as I let my light so shine before men, that they see my good work, and glorify our Father in heaven. And remember, our love for God strengthens our love for each other. As your relationship with the Father grows, our oneness increases, and I feel your presence always, in all ways. I

Johnny Ellis #374452

love you, Honey!

Wednesday, April 26, 2000

Hi Sweetie,
    Thank you for the beautiful Easter card.
    Dear Husband, how is your journey within? Have you begun to consciously look inside to discover just what God put in you? Ask the Lord to reveal to you your true purpose, your role in this life, at this time, with me. Let me know what He tells you. I love you, Sweetie. Time is meaningless when our love is eternal.

Johnny Ellis #374452

MAY, 2000

Sunday, May 14, 2000

Dearest Husband,
Happy Birthday to you, my Love.
But the Helper, the Holy Spirit, whom the Father will send in My name, He will teach you all things and bring to your remembrance <u>all things that I said to you</u>. John 14:26
Blessed is she who believed, for there will be a fulfillment of <u>those things which were told her from the Lord.</u> Luke 1:45
And the Lord said, "Shall I hide from Abraham what I am doing, since Abraham shall surely become a great and mighty nation, and all the nations of the earth shall be blessed in him? For I have known him, in order that he may command his children and his household after him, that they keep the way of the Lord, to do righteousness and justice, that the Lord may bring to Abraham <u>what He has spoken to him</u>." Genesis 18:17-19
And the Scripture, foreseeing that God would justify the nations by faith, <u>preached the gospel to Abraham beforehand, saying, "In you all the nations shall be blessed</u>." Galatians 3:8
Henceforth, all generations will call me blessed. Luke 1:48
John, God has given me exceedingly and great promises. I am she who believes, so that He can do all that He has revealed to me. Yes, you are a part of the plan, a very great and wonderful part. Are you ready to be all that God has created you to be? Are you finished hiding the beauty of your soul? Do you feel like my Husband? Are your hands open and empty, ready to receive all of God's blessings?
I have definitely reached a turning point, a new plateau in my life, and I am going forward in harmony with God's will for me. You will not be left behind. God promised me, and I believe. Are you ready for signs and wonders? Just let Him have His way with you. Remember, its God's plan, not ours. *Eye has not seen, and ear has not heard the things that He has prepared for us!* So get ready to be surprised and amazed. *Nothing is too hard for the Lord.* I love you, Sweetie. Keep looking within, and you will find all the answers there. That's where Jesus said the Kingdom is. Do you believe? Then get ready to receive!

Johnny Ellis #374452

Thursday, May 18, 2000

Hi Sweetie,
    Thank you for your letter of May 14. It is filled with so many beautiful thoughts. As for you, you expressed your faith in God's plan for you. You said He is revealing His plan to you. Please share with me as you awaken to His will. We all have a specific function to fulfill, to do our part in bringing the Kingdom of God to earth. Discovering our part is the greatest adventure imaginable. But first, we must completely let go of our old self-image. We must admit that we don't know who we are. Then the slate is clean for God to reveal His design for our lives.
    In March, 1984, I fully realized that I was unhappy with my life as I was living it. I turned to the Lord, and asked Him to let me be "all that I am," that is, all that He created me to be, since, in my heart I knew that there must be more to life than I was experiencing at that time. John, I never heard you say that you didn't like your life when you were destroying yourself with drugs and alcohol. In fact, you made it clear that this was what you wanted, what you enjoyed. Now, because of circumstances, you are unable to live the life of your choice, so you are talking about God and a life with me. But, what happens when you get out of prison? What happens when the things you really love are accessible to you once again?
    Can you answer my questions? Based on past experience, no matter how much I did for you, you still ended up choosing your old life instead of me. Why should this time be any different? No matter how much I love you, or what I can see and do for you, why should I lift one finger for you, and then watch you go down that old road again, without me? So, whatever you desire, *seek ye first the Kingdom of God and His righteousness,* and I will be there. Or seek your old ways, and I won't be a part of it. This is an inside job, John. God knows your heart. Only you can decide which way you will go.
    I have a drawer filled with nearly ten years of your letters expressing everything I wanted to hear. But it didn't mean a thing. So, this time, before I get excited, SHOW ME! That means complete transformation, in the name of Jesus. When Christ lives in you completely, I'm sure I will know it. There will be signs and wonders, and you will be standing by my side, through no effort on

Johnny Ellis #374452

my part. I am totally obedient to the Holy Spirit of God, so I know that when my part is revealed, I will perform it perfectly. Right now, God is perfecting me for my role in bringing the Kingdom to earth.

We must be Selfish now, that is, we must focus on becoming our higher Selves. It took me many years to learn this. Don't worry about me anymore. Grab onto the Lord with both hands, and promise to never let go, just as He promised to always be with you. Remember, it's God's plan, and what He wills will come to pass. We can only delay it. Let's not waste any more time. Simply demand that God reveal His plan for you now. Then begin to experience who you are and why you were born, according to God's will, by the power of the Holy Spirit, in the name of our Lord and Savior, Jesus Christ. It's so simple. It's time for the lowly caterpillar to become a beautiful butterfly. Come, let's fly away together. I love you.

Monday, May 29, 2000

Hi Sweetie,

Happy Memorial Day! I'll always remember you. It was so good to hear your voice over the weekend. And it was wonderful to pray with you. The deeper I get into the Word of God, the more confident I become of His promises. When two join together in the name of Jesus, there is power. Everything we prayed for **is.** We may not doubt, but need only to believe. I believe, Honey. The past cannot touch us when we are fully surrendered to God. He is completely in charge. As long as we love Him and are willing and obedient, everything is working together for good. Believe. Receive.

You can be sure I stay in prayer all day long. My connection to God keeps getting stronger and clearer. When I pray in tongues, I receive visions. We are both living one day at a time, but right now, I feel that I am ready for anything! Whatever comes my way, I have confidence that the Holy Spirit will direct me.

*And the Lord your God will circumcise your heart and the heart of your descendants to **love** the Lord your God with all your heart and with all your soul, **that you may live.*** Deuteronomy 30:6

*I command you today to **love** the Lord your God, to walk in His ways, and to keep His commandments, His statutes, and*

Johnny Ellis #374452

*His judgments, **that you may live.*** Deuteronomy 30:16
Choose life, *that both you and your descendants may **live**; that you may **love** the Lord your God, that you may obey His voice, and that you may **cling to Him** for **He is your life**.* Deuteronomy 30:19-20
God is not the God of the dead, but of the living. Matthew 22:32
*Let those who **love** Him be like the sun when it comes out in full strength.* Judges 5:31

John, based on the above Scriptures, when we love God, we choose life. The two are inseparable. So just keep loving the Lord, with all your heart, soul, mind and strength. Bring every thought in line with His Word. Consider how God has loved you and blessed you in your life, regardless of the choices you have made. Fall in love with God, John. Be His man. Let the light of His love shine through you. Give your whole self to God. Let David show you how in the Psalms. He was a man after God's own heart. Love God!

Choose Life! Now, right where you are. When you get "this moment" right, the future will take care of itself. This moment is the only time that you can make a change, a change of heart and mind. Don't even think about the past or the future. Give your whole self to this moment. Speak in tongues when you don't know what to pray. It is powerful. It isn't difficult, Honey. It's easy. Just make up your mind. That's all.

When you go to bed tonight, rest in God's arms. Let Him love you, comfort you, and He will strengthen you and prepare you for His plan. It really is easy. I love you.

Johnny Ellis #374452

JUNE, 2000

Tuesday evening, June 13, 200

Hi, Honey. Happy Father's Day!
　　As you know, Sunday, Father's Day, is my graduation. I too will be wearing a cap and gown. I don't expect anyone to be there for me, except God, Jesus, and the Holy Spirit.
　　I'm having fun. I'm reading the Bible through, but not cover to cover. I started with Genesis, Revelation, Epistles of James, Peter, John, and Jude, and today I'm reading Hebrews. The Word is so alive in me now. In the name of Jesus, I claim the kind of ministry He spoke of in Mark 16, where the Word will be confirmed with signs and wonders. I won't settle for less. He promised me that.
　　Are you ready for some freedom? When you have freedom again, will you treasure it? Will you appreciate each moment, and use it for God's glory? And when you have me in your arms again, will you treasure me, and love and appreciate every moment we are together?

Thursday, June 22, 2000

Hi, Honey!
　　John, I know that you have made tremendous leaps spiritually. When I wrote those "X-rated" comments on the back of the envelope, I had the letter in my purse when I went to church. I "saw" you there, "felt" your spirit, and the tears began to flow. This has happened before, and again since. Last Sunday, at the beginning of the service, before my graduation, I again "saw" you and the tears again flowed. Remember, a while back, I wrote that I saw a man walking on the other side of the street, and I "saw" your face on him. I got into my car, and the tears fell like rain. Also, when the Spirit led me to that card, I stood in the store and the tears flowed. This is evidence of your spirit being fully present with me and the love we have for each other.
　　This past week, even the children have begun asking about you. "Where's John? When will we see him again?" So I know that you are reaching us all in the spirit. Keep loving God, and sending your love to us. It is powerful. Love IS the greatest

Johnny Ellis #374452

power in the world. Love heals. Love is the glue that keeps us connected. Together, in love, there is nothing we cannot accomplish for God and mankind. What a joy to serve the Lord together! So keep growing in your knowledge of the Lord. The more we have, the more we can give. The more we give, the more we have! Receive from the Lord, and give to all around. Send love to everyone in that prison, guards as well as inmates, from the strongest to the weakest, from the most powerful, to the meekest. And then see how that love comes back to you in surprising and amazing ways. This is how God works. We must give to receive.

I'm glad you liked my sermon. There's a lot more where that came from. I've learned to make my poems more powerful with relevant Scripture. I love you, Honey!

Wednesday, June 28, 2000

Hi Sweetie!

John, when we both get this right, following the Holy Spirit day and night, doors will open, and we will demonstrate a power, a love, and a joy the world has never yet seen. Are you with me in this?

John, I am really excited about the prospects the Spirit is showing me, because none of this would be happening if you were not getting right with God. Nothing thrills me more than the thought of my true husband, manifested in the flesh, just as God created you to be. I love you, Sweetheart. God reminds me to think only on what is true, and lovely, and perfect, and I remember all of the beautiful time we have shared, how I loved to touch you, and lick you, how my heart swelled with joy seeing you relate to people, seeing how people responded to you, seeing the God-given qualities you possess manifested in our lives.

Are you ready to resist the old habits, and give yourself entirely over to God's plan for our lives? It's a moment by moment choice, and I'm here to help you make it, as your wife, your friend, your partner on every level, spiritually, mentally, emotionally, and physically. Eye has not seen, and ear has not heard the things that God has planned for us. He will do exceedingly, abundantly above anything we could ask, think, or imagine.

When I presented my sermon, one of my classmates heard the Holy Spirit say that I was going to be extremely wealthy. The

Johnny Ellis #374452

Spirit has been putting the words "multi-billionaire" in my mind. Are you ready for this? Do you think you could handle all the love, joy, peace, prosperity and much more that God wants us to enjoy? If so, begin right now to claim it, and praise and thank God for all His blessings. Is anything too hard for the Lord? With God, all things are possible. Our willingness is all He needs. He is putting everything into place.
    I love you, Honey!

Johnny Ellis #374452

Johnny Ellis #374452

JULY, 2000

Sunday afternoon, July 2, 2000

Hi Sweetie!

I just hung up the phone, and came right over to the computer to continue the flow of our conversation. Your voice sounds sooooooo good to me. You are the sweetest man in the whole world. I'm so glad you're mine! Now, let's keep it that way. Remember 2 Peter 2:20-22 (that's a lot of twos).

Since you are mature in the Lord, to turn away from Him now would be spiritual suicide. You are an intelligent, loving, wonderful, sanctified, anointed human being. Anyone can make a mistake, but only a fool would repeat it, and you're NO FOOL! So, stay in the Word, keep God in your heart, on your mind, and on your lips and tongue.

Speaking of tongues: *The tongue of the righteous is choice silver.* (Proverbs 10:20) *The tongue of the wise promotes health.* (Proverbs 12:18) *A wholesome tongue is a tree of life.* (Proverbs 15:4) *Death and life are in the power of the tongue, and those who love it will eat its fruit.* (Proverbs 18:21) *She opens her mouth with wisdom, and on her tongue is the law of kindness.* (Proverbs 31:26) *Your lips, O my spouse, drip as the honeycomb; honey and milk are under your tongue.* (Song of Solomon 4:11)

John, God has put me back in your corner. I never want to leave again, but you know, it is totally up to you. Keep making the right choices, and we will never be apart. Think "MINISTRY!" Just be yourself, and you will be serving God. By the time you get out, we will have so much testimony, it will take forever for us to tell it all.

John, we must trust the Holy Spirit of God. His plan is perfect, but we will miss it if we try to make our own way. And we can hear His voice only when we are still, and seeking to know God's perfect will for us. The only way for us to stay in harmony with each other, is for each of us to stay in perfect harmony with God. There is no other way.

In my studies, I learned a very important distinction: God's permissive will, and God's Perfect Will. Because God gave us free will, he allows us to make our own choices, as when you decided to spend your life back on the streets. This is your decision to

Johnny Ellis #374452

make. God will not interfere. I now know that I also may not interfere. All that I can do is to keep loving you from a distance. When we are following the world and not God, we are in His permissive will, even if it leads us to hell. In order to be in His Perfect Will, we must seek Him day and night, pray without ceasing, and love Him with our whole heart, soul, mind and body. Are you doing that, John? If not, are you ready to begin? We must go all the way with God. We can't serve two masters. I know that you tried hard to do that. See where it got you. God wants your all. He won't settle for less, and neither will I. I love you, Honey.

Saturday afternoon, July 8, 2000

Hi Sweetie!

Still waiting for the mail. Meanwhile, I'll write what has been on my mind for the past few days. It's my concern for your immortal soul. God has been merciful to you, even though you have thumbed your nose at Him. Please don't think you can go on pretending you are a Christian, while loving the things of the world that please you. No matter how much God loves you, or how much I love you, only you can make the choice which way you will go. God will not violate His Own Word. I have tried to step in to rescue you from hell, but I have finally learned that I may not. So, dearest husband, it's up to you.

However, I can quote Scripture that may enter into your heart, mind, and soul to help you to make the only sane decision, the decision to choose life rather than death, to choose light rather than darkness, to choose all the wonderful gifts that God has for you. Even if you weren't my husband, I would still wish this for you. So let's read:

Hebrews 6:4-6 *For **it is impossible** for those who were once enlightened, and have tasted the heavenly gift (Jesus), and have become partakers of the Holy Spirit, and have tasted the good word of God and the powers of the age to come, **if they fall away, to renew them again to repentance**, since they crucify again for themselves the Son of God, and put Him to an open shame.*

Hebrews 10:26-29 *For **if we sin willfully** after we have received the knowledge of the truth, **there no longer remains a sacrifice for sins**, but a certain fearful expectation of judgment,* *and fiery indignation which will devour the adversaries. Anyone who has rejected Moses' law dies without mercy on the testimony of two or three witnesses. Of how much worse punishment, do you suppose, will he be thought worthy who has trampled the Son of God underfoot, counted the blood of the covenant by which he was sanctified a common thing, and insulted the Spirit of grace?*

    2 Peter 2:20-22 *For if, after they have escaped the pollutions of the world through the knowledge of the Lord and Savior Jesus Christ,* **they are again entangled** *in them and overcome, the latter end is worse for them than the beginning. For it would have been better for them not to have known the way of righteousness, than having known it, to turn from the holy commandment delivered to them. But it has happened to them according to the true proverb: "A dog returns to his own vomit," and, "a sow, having washed, to her wallowing in the mire."*

    1 John 5:16 *If anyone sees his brother sinning a sin which does not lead to death, he will ask, and He will give him life for those who commit sin not leading to death. There is sin leading to (spiritual) death. I do not say that he should pray about that.*

    John, I have prayed for you day and night since we met. But last summer, when you returned to the filth of the streets, God told me to take my hands off of you. That's when I began locking the door on you. I had to sit back and watch you go down the road leading to death. God truly is merciful. You would not have lived very long if you hadn't gone to prison. Choose life, John, not for me, but for yourself. One soul more or less in hell won't make any difference to hell, but what a difference it will make to that soul, who by its own free will, finds itself in the eternal fire. Especially after God has shown such favor to that soul, offering every good and perfect gift to it. Don't let that happen to you, Honey. I now know how to let go, so I will go on. But, I still have hope that we can go on together, in God's perfect will.

    I do love you.

Johnny Ellis #374452

*Then Samuel took the horn of oil and **anointed him** in the midst of his brothers; and the Spirit of the Lord came upon David from that day forward.* 1 Samuel 16:13 *But the Spirit of the Lord departed from Saul, and a distressing spirit from the Lord troubled him.* 1 Samuel 16:14 The title Christ signifies "The Anointed One."

Thursday, July 13, 2000

John,
   You can see from the above Scriptures, that the anointing is given, and it is also taken away. These pictures demonstrate the outward manifestation. You definitely demonstrated your anointing when you spoke at the graduation in 1996. People were deeply moved by your words. Of course, the other pictures were taken shortly before your incarceration. Any fool can see the difference. You sold your soul to Satan. Have you fully reclaimed it? Are you really finished with that life? I am.
   Do not be unequally yoked together with unbelievers. For what fellowship has righteousness with lawlessness? And what communion has light with darkness? And what accord has Christ with Belial? Or what part has a believer with an unbeliever? And

Johnny Ellis #374452

what agreement has the temple of God with idols? For you are the temple of the living God. 2 Corinthians 6:14-16

Come out from among them and be separate, says the Lord. Do not touch what is unclean, and I will receive you. 2 Corinthians 6:17

I have seen you with the anointing, and I have seen you throw it away. Choose, John, choose. As for me, I choose to serve the Lord.

*Then Jesus said to him, "Away with you, Satan! For it is written, 'You shall worship the Lord your God, and Him **only** you shall serve.'"* Matthew 4:10

My desire is for the Lord. My heart's desire is to serve Him, and to move forward with my ministry. I have been making Johnny Ellis a priority in my life. I am now faced with a choice. Looking back over our nearly ten years together, I see that I fulfilled my purpose in your life, to lift you up to the Lord. I have seen the anointing on you, and nothing in this life has ever thrilled me more.

You, of your own free will, threw away God's precious gift. So, only you, of your own free will can, by God's grace, receive it back again, while you have life and breath. This is probably your last chance in this life to totally surrender to the Lord, and be all that He created you to be. My letters are filled with exhortation to awaken you to God's will in your life. I have done all that I can. Now, it's up to you. May God be with you.
Saturday, July 15, 2000

Dear John,

I do pray without ceasing, constantly seeking the Lord's will. The more I do to try to help you, the less you have to do. Yes, I have given my all to you all these years, but what difference did it really make? You did not choose to be with me when you had the freedom to do so. We would be together now if it was what you really wanted. You single-handedly created your situation. The thought of trying to help you again only to have you go back to the filth is totally depressing. I can't do that to myself again.

Jesus is my Lord. Jesus is my Bridegroom. Jesus is my Lover. Jesus is my All. What is Jesus to you? Look inside, John. He told me He would come to me as a "Dark Thief." Are you the One, or must I look for another? Bury yourself in Scripture. That's where you will find true freedom. That's where you will find your

Johnny Ellis #374452

Self!
John, you once said that I should go forward with my ministry and you would catch up with me. Maybe that was prophetic. The visiting situation will take care of itself in time. The important thing is that we each sit at the Lord's feet, and take in all we can of His Word, His blessings, His anointing, His love, all the things He gives us so freely.

There is no earthly man for me except you. But you must choose to be all that God created you to be. I can no longer settle for less. I have come too far. So I will focus my whole heart, soul, mind, and strength on the Lord.

Honey, don't think that I love you less. We haven't experienced being husband and wife for quite a while now, because of your choice to serve Satan. I don't know if you remember, but, one time, when I drove to Madison to see you, I came in and sat down across the table from "you" and I demanded to know, "Where is my husband?" Looking into your eyes, I saw Satan. Using your voice, he told me I'd better leave in a hurry or you might hurt me. I immediately left, and as I was driving back home, I asked the Lord why I had driven all that way, only to turn around right away to drive back. The Lord told me that it was necessary for me to see you that way. During the year before your imprisonment, whenever we were together intimately, I would end up with something unpleasant.   I am a patient woman, John, and I have faith. God has made me exceedingly great promises regarding you. Only your total love and surrender to God can allow them to become reality. My part now is to go forward in the ministry. I love you.

Monday, July 17, 2000

Dear John,
I repent, and turn from all my transgressions, so that iniquity will not be my ruin. I cast away from myself all the transgressions which I have committed, and get myself a new heart and a new spirit. For why should I die? The Lord God has no pleasure in the death of one who dies. Therefore I turn and live. Ezekiel 18:30-32

I am swift to hear, slow to speak, slow to wrath, for my wrath does not produce the righteousness of God. Therefore I lay aside all filthiness and overflow of wickedness, and I receive with

Johnny Ellis #374452

meekness the implanted word, which is able to save my soul. I am a doer of the word, and not a hearer only. I will not deceive myself. James 1:19-22

Sweetheart, I AM A DOER OF THE WORD! And I have discovered that by putting Scripture in the first person, present tense, it's much easier to be a doer of the Word. Then, when we read aloud, we know that we are talking about ourselves, here and now, and not someone else out there. So that's what I did to Ezekiel 18:30-32, a very appropriate verse for you at this time. How did you find it? Now I know for sure that the Holy Spirit is working in your life. God does not want you to die, and neither do I. I want what God wants, and He has a beautiful plan for you and me for eternity. Keep looking inside. It's all there.

The Helper, the Holy Spirit, whom the Father has sent in Jesus' name, He teaches me all things, and brings to my remembrance all things that Jesus said to me. John 14:26

Last night you came to me, and we made passionate love. I heard your voice, and I felt you. Our spirits are one, Honey. Stay in the word. That is your only protection from backsliding again. I don't want to lose you. By "letting go" of you, God can better guide us both to the fulfillment of His plan for us.

I come to Jesus, laboring and heavy laden, and He gives me rest. I take His yoke upon myself and learn from Him, for He is gentle and lowly in heart, and I find rest for my soul. For His yoke is easy and His burden is light. Matthew 11:28-30

I humble myself under the mighty hand of God, that He may exalt me in due time, casting all my care upon Him, for He cares for me. 1 Peter 5:6-7

So, I guess what I'm saying when I "let go," is that I'm giving the situation over to God. Suddenly, everything looks different. Priorities are rearranged. We were making our visits a priority, when I didn't really know if you will return to the streets when you are out. Something in my spirit made me uneasy about putting my effort into the visits. And so I "let go." I backed up from "laboring" for the visits. Then Jesus was able to let me know that he needs ALL of my attention to be focused on Him. Then guess what? He has me writing to you again, and again, more than before!

Something wonderful is going on, John. His yoke IS easy. When we find ourselves trying too hard, we need to let go, and let God redirect us. Otherwise our path becomes blocked, and even

Johnny Ellis #374452

our feelings can be blocked. Right now, my love for you is flowing in torrents. Jesus is the director of my love, because I gave it all to Him. He wants you to have it. He wants you to have me! But you must continue to do your part, to be obedient to the Word of God. Let the Holy Spirit of God continue to guide you. I will do the same. We can't miss. Our love will light up the world! I love you.

Saturday, July 22, 2000

Dear Johnny,
      Just a quick report after Corporate Prayer. I had my manuscript, music, etc. in a bag, and I brought it to Church, to ask for prayer and direction for my ministry. During the group prayer, I was lifting various people up in prayer, as the Holy Spirit brought them to my mind. When I presented you to God, I heard the words, "the Christ, the Christ, the Christ, Johnny Ellis is the Christ." And while praying for my ministry, I heard that my ministry to you was the most important aspect of my ministry.
      Is anything too hard for the Lord? God makes a way where there is no way. With God, all things are possible.

Johnny Ellis #374452

AUGUST, 2000

Monday morning, August 7, 2000

Hi Sweetie!
    We are both waking up, waking up to God's plan for our lives which no one or nothing can ever take from us as long as we both desire it, believe it can be, and lay hold of it with our faith. When I see you next, I plan to listen to you and hear you tell me all that is in your heart, especially your plans and desires for our life together. I love you.

Johnny Ellis #374452

Johnny Ellis #374452

SEPTEMBER, 2000

Saturday night, September 2, 2000

Hi, Sweetie!
Today I received your letter of August 30, and you asked for some encouraging news, "a spirit booster." Well, I decided to come into your bed tonight. How's that! I hope that you enjoy it. I will write more in the morning. I do love you!!!

Monday morning, September 4, 2000

For there is nothing covered that will not be revealed, nor hidden that will not be known. Luke 12:2
A certain man had a fig tree planted in his vineyard and he came seeking fruit on it and found none. Then he said to the keeper of his vineyard,
"Look, for three years I have come seeking fruit on this fig tree and find none. Cut it down; why does it use up the ground?"
But she answered and said to him,
"Sir, let it alone this year also, until I dig around it and fertilize it. And if it bears fruit, well. But if not, after that you can cut it down." Luke 13:6-9

John, God is the owner of the above vineyard, you are the fig tree, and I am the keeper of the vineyard. By inspiration of the Holy Spirit, I continually pour out fertilization on you, so you will not be cut down. Are you ready to bear fruit? Are you ready to review your life (lives) and realize the journey of your soul? Are you ready to discover your true purpose, why God has preserved your life all these years in spite of your choices?

Oh, my love, I pray for you in my heart without ceasing. Choose to be all that God created you to be. The path will open to you. Do not worry, or be dismayed or cast down. Know that your Redeemer lives, right in your very heart. Let your light so shine that men see your good works, that our Father may be glorified.

Honey, this is a time for boldness. We must be bold in our believing as we grasp God's Truth for us. We cannot afford to be wimps. Remember, eye has not seen and ear has not heard the things that He has prepared for us. He does exceedingly, abundantly above anything we can imagine. With God, all things

Johnny Ellis #374452

are possible.
    Think of Joseph, so many years in that Egyptian prison. Upon his release, he was made ruler of all the land. Oh, John, I want to give the world to you. God wants to give the world to you! You must reach out and take it. Reach out with your whole heart, soul, mind, and strength. No one can do this for you. See yourself receiving all that God has for you. See yourself fulfilling His plan for you. You will see me by your side always, to love you, to comfort you, to support you, always.

Friday, September 29, 2000

Hi Sweetie,
    I recently had a bad dream. I dreamt that you came out of prison and we were together. You kissed me four times, and then I looked around and you were gone, along with my car and my few dollars. I was completely lost, not knowing what to do. Then came a phone call. I recognized your voice, but you were completely out of your mind. When I woke up I prayed, and bound any spirit of doubt and fear within me. I also bound any spirits of addiction and insanity that may have had an eye on you.
    Last Tuesday I answered the phone and it sounded like a call from you, but it was cut off. Of course I would have accepted it. Did you hang up? The answering machine caught your call on Monday, when I wasn't home. I had fun playing the beginning over and over and listening to "Johnny Ellis," "Johnny Ellis," "Johnny Ellis." At least I got to hear your voice for free!
    I know for sure that everything I have done on your behalf could only have been done by the grace of God, and not in my own strength. I never could have found you on my own. And I never would have recognized you as my husband without God's prompting.
    And the only thing that could possibly explain the depth of my love for you is that we are two souls who have loved before, many times in many ways over eons of time into eternity. Do you know that, John? Are you beginning to be conscious of our true relationship to each other? Please ask the Holy Spirit to reveal all to you. The more we know about each other, the more we can appreciate our true relationship, created by God for His glory. I love you forever.

Johnny Ellis #374452

DECEMBER, 2000

Wednesday, December 20, 2000

To my Precious Love,
    I write to you now in prayer, according to the will of God Most High, by the power of the Holy Spirit, in the name of our precious Lord and Savior Jesus Christ. I seek not my own will, which is to be with you eternally. I seek God's will to be clearly revealed that we may obey with certainty.
    Yesterday, after I visited you, I had just turned onto Interstate 90 from 151. Cars were coming from the ramp from East Town Mall in Madison. Right before my eyes a car flipped over, and the car behind him missed me by inches. We both pulled over. I called "911" on my cell phone, and the other driver ran back to see if the occupant of the flipped car was all right. He was able to get out of the flipped car and walk, but he was as white as this paper. Remember, Honey, that we prayed for all the drivers. God is so merciful. This could easily have turned into a three car accident. I don't even remember what I did, but the other driver said he was thankful that I saw him, as he had no place else to go but in my lane.
    As you can imagine, I kept seeing this car flipping over, like a toy, as I drove home. Even though the roads looked dry, there were patches of ice ready to create an accident. This morning, in my prayer time, I asked the Lord what I was to learn from yesterday...the big accident that caused me to sit in my car for two hours on the way to Waupun, and this car flipping right before my eyes. I immediately opened my Bible and read Ezekiel 24:16,18, "Son of man, behold, I take away from you the desire of your eyes with one strike." "At evening my wife died."
    More snow is predicted. I love you with all my heart, but I will not be coming to see you until God gives me the "all clear" sign. John, I asked you yesterday if you could imagine that you would ever want to get away from me. I believe that God wants you to make a vow to Him, to me, and to our marriage, that you will never again put the streets, drugs, and other women before our marriage. Otherwise he might just as well take me from you now, as He did Ezekiel.
    I send you "Love and Memories" for Christmas and our

Johnny Ellis #374452

Tenth Anniversary. We must learn our lessons from the less-than-lovely memories, so that we can let them go. There are more than enough beautiful memories to let me know that you are the only man in the universe for me. Perhaps God, in His Wisdom, needs us to be separate for a little while so He can transform us completely. When we are together, I do feel the heat building up within me. My love for you cannot be contained forever. You are so beautiful to me, and the beauty you see in me is but your own reflection smiling back at you. Do you know how beautifully and wonderfully God has made you? I see it all, and thank God that you are my husband. We are truly one, you, me and God. Do you know what power lies in that Oneness? Let us claim that power in the universe to do God's will now and forever. Let us cleanse every dark corner in our hearts, souls and minds, so that when we are together again, it will be forever.

As you said, we light up a room with our love. Now God would have us light up the world. As my poem says,
> I want the world to know our glow.
> Our love's ablaze. It lights the evening sky.
> A beacon bright that others may travel by.
> Oh Jesus, I want the world to know.

Monday, December 25, 2000

To my Sweetheart on Christmas Day,

Even though we have not been together physically this past week, please know that your dear spirit is in all that I do...even in the gifts that I give. I told you that my Dad has the beautiful crucifix that you made in his bedroom, and my Mom has the Virgin Mary vase with silk roses displayed in a prominent place in the living room.

Now, for Christmas everyone in the family that I see will receive a copy of this picture of Jesus with the Roses that you sent to me. There is such a wonderful and powerful anointing on that picture, especially the words, "Jesus, I trust in you." But, most of all, it combines your love for me with the love of Christ for both of us. Often it seems that Jesus is stepping out of the picture, truly giving me the gift of the rose, which I now see signifies my very life. And as I drive on the treacherous highways, the words rise out of my very soul, "Jesus, I trust in you." Oh, that the whole world

Johnny Ellis #374452

would learn to say these words...that all of mankind will call upon his Holy Name, and be saved.

You are in all that I do. As we both grow spiritually, our lives intertwine and grow more beautiful, just as the roses in the picture. Yes, we are flowers of God's design, unable to open by our own power. But how sweetly God unfolds each petal, as we "trust Him to unfold the moments of our lives just as He unfolds the rose."

I brought copies of the picture to "Corporate prayer" Saturday morning, and gave one each to a group of saints who prayed with me for confirmation that God might want me to use this picture in my ministry. One lady told me that she had been a drug addict, and one day she dreamt of a coffin with a cross of roses on the lid. The coffin opened, and she saw herself rise out of it, alive. That was the end of her addiction. She was thrilled to get the picture. Pictures play a great role in the beliefs of Catholics. Perhaps this is one way that I will reach them for Jesus. Also, it will replace that myth that Jesus is a fair haired person.

John, as I write this letter, the Holy Spirit unfolds more and more of His plan for us and shows me new ways to proclaim the works of the Lord. "One picture is worth a thousand words." The rose is very significant in this end time of preparation for His second coming. It speaks to the heart of His people. Please ask the artist if this would be all right with him for me to distribute copies of this picture. Also, I am enclosing copies for you to share.

Where did you get the poem, "the Rose." I would like to share that also, even in my speaking engagements. It says so beautifully God's role in our lives. John, even in prison, you are my partner, contributing to my life and making it more beautiful. God hears our every prayer. Our faith brings it all to fruition NOW. Yes, everything we ask, believing, happens on the spiritual level immediately. Then it is just a matter of time for it to manifest into our physical lives. As we practice our faith, the time element diminishes and disappears, and we begin to have results as we speak and believe. This is miracle power, signs and wonders to be displayed in the earth for God's glory. *For the eyes of the Lord run to and fro throughout the whole earth, to show Himself strong on behalf of those whose heart is loyal to Him.* 2 Chronicles 16:9. God wants to "show Himself strong" in our life, Honey. Yes, our life, one life, yours, mine, and the Holy Spirit of God, ever united as One, glorious, victorious forever. God honors and rewards our

Johnny Ellis #374452

obedience to Him. I love you.

Johnny Ellis #374452

Thursday, December 28, 2000

Hi, Sweetheart! Happy New Year!!
    As the year quickly comes to a close, I will write to you one more time in the year 2000. Thank you for the beautiful gifts you have made. The angels are adorable, the unicorn is very handsome and majestic, and the heart container is very, very pretty. I think you must have discovered that "less is more" when it comes to these works of art. The more simple, the lovelier they are.
    The same is true of us. The less we try to manipulate our own lives, the more the true beauty of God's creation shines through, just like the Rose. We have learned many lessons this year. Most of all, we are learning to trust God in all things. His plan is perfect. He simply needs us not to interfere, but to follow in perfect faith, knowing that His way is exceedingly, abundantly, above and beyond anything we could think or imagine. I find this very exciting. I could never go back to trying to plan things my own way. He keeps us and guides us every step of the way. When we choose to follow His way, we are completely provided for, every moment.
    It is God's will for us to be together. I have no doubt of that. Therefore, we needn't struggle or put forth great effort for this to come to pass. All we must do is to tune into His voice moment to moment, and to be totally obedient. The Holy Spirit will deal with any thoughts left over from the "old man." All we have to do is to be willing to let go.
    Everything I do is preparing the way for us to be together. No matter how often I come to see you, I am with you always in love, and in your heart. And you are with me, in my heart. As we seek the Lord, to know Him better, to know His will for us, our love for each other unfolds, like the petals of the Rose.
    Do you remember Lord Krsna? He is called the Supreme Personality of Godhead. I am re-reading the Bhagavad-Gita (As It Is) in which the Lord speaks to His friend, Arjuna, and explains our eternal relationship to Him. He says, "The one with great faith who always abides in Me, thinks of Me within himself, and renders transcendental loving service to Me is the most intimately united with Me and is the highest of all. That is My opinion." Since studying the Bible, it is clearer to me than ever that Lord Krsna is

Johnny Ellis #374452

the Lord Jesus Christ. As Krsna, He appeared four thousand years ago, and at that time He promised to come back in the physical to remind us of our eternal relationship with Him, and to remind us that He lives in our hearts always.

Krsna is clearly identified as incarnating as a black man, and His eternal consort (wife) is Radha, a white woman. In the Book of Genesis it says, "Let Us make mankind in Our image, according to Our likeness.....Male and female He created them (Genesis 1:26-27). The image of God as male and female is not referred to after that in the Bible, but I see clearly that Krsna with Radha is the image of God. There is much to be learned from studying this couple. We have much in common with them! I'm going to send for a book that refers to them. I'll share what I learn with you.

We are on such an exciting path. Watching our lives unfold, seeing how the Lord is in charge of it all, anticipating what will happen next, fills me with joy. Right where you are, you are blossoming and growing in the way the Lord would have you grow. Rejoice and be glad that you hear His voice. You had made a wrong choice. He had to slow you down and get you alone, so that you could be restored to your right mind, and make a better choice, the choice to be all that God created you to be. I love you.

Johnny Ellis #374452

JANUARY, 2001

3:39 a.m., Saturday Morning, January 20, 2001

Hi Sweetheart!
 I just turned on the radio and heard the song, "Spanish Guitar." *Play me like a Spanish guitar. Hold me in your arms all night long. I'll be your song.* I am your song. My soft panting is a beautiful song to your ears, as you play me, as you play on every part of me.
 Oh, John, yesterday, when I asked you to imagine leaving with me, you took me with you. I was completely transported out of the earthly reality to a place where you and I were alone together. I have told you that my home is in your arms. Yesterday, during our visit, I saw my whole world in your eyes. You are my very life. I love you.
 We are a unique couple, able to communicate on every level, heart, soul, mind, spirit, and body. We are truly one. To experience this sweet oneness is heaven on earth. Everything else, our life, our ministry grows out of this Oneness. Our love will spread over the whole world, awakening the Oneness of all human beings. Our "work,' our mission in this life is simply to love each other completely. What a job!
 Joy is power, and yesterday the experience of joy was intensified to a new level. Yes, My Love, yesterday, you took me to a new level, right there, in your eyes. I am a happy woman, happy being totally in love with my Husband. Love is power. We are a powerful couple. Is there anything we cannot achieve? Absolutely not!! As we reach out with our minds for everything our hearts desire, it will be drawn to us. Yes, every good, and beautiful, and perfect thing that we desire will come to us. Number One on the list is our togetherness. As our union on the spiritual, mental, and emotional level grows and intensifies, our physical union cannot be far behind. Believe. Receive.
 I know that you are with me, and that your prayers for me empower all that I do. You are my true partner, friend, lover, husband, my ALL. Thank you, God Most High, for bringing Johnny Louis Ellis into my life. My greatest desire was for a partner to love me totally, for all eternity. Now that I have fully realized my greatest desire, it's just glory after glory. Having you as my true

Johnny Ellis #374452

Husband gives me a foundation, the fulfillment of my most important desire.

Monday morning, January 29, 2001

Hi Sweetie!
    Right now I see wonderful things happening in your life...wonderful opportunities for you to blossom and grow. I'm so proud of you. We are both on the path of growth. When we are together again, I believe that it will be a win/win relationship. The proverbial "hole in your bucket" is being healed. Yes, the drugs and alcohol drained your life force from you just like having a hole in your soul, and because we are one, I too was damaged by your choices. There is no room in our lives for this nonsense. Know that the Holy Spirit of God gives you everything you need to support your choice to be finished with this life.
    I'm looking forward to the marriage enrichment seminar sessions. I guess that the most important thing I'll be looking for is to understand if you have really made this choice for yourself. Even if I wasn't in your life, would you still want to live for the Lord? I realize more and more that this is an inside job. It can't be dependent on anyone else except our personal relationship with God. Seek first the kingdom of God and His righteousness, and all these things (our marriage and ministry) will be added to it.
    In the past, when you just "thought" it was over between us, you immediately fell back into the drugs and the arms of some filthy bitch. The pain and disappointment of my "husband" going down this path, and the possibility of it happening again is something that we must deal with. No matter how much I love you, you have to change from the inside, you have to want a better life for yourself, to love yourself, before you can be a strong partner to me.
    Examine your thoughts each moment. Every doubt, every fear, every angry, negative thought will bring you right back on the path of destruction. Only you can choose your thoughts. Only you can put on the mind of Christ, and let Him give you His thoughts, and teach you His ways.
    John, I didn't know that I was going to write this, to deal with this in my letter to you. When we are together, I love being with you. But, I am extremely sensitive in what I perceive, and

Johnny Ellis #374452

there seems to still be a darkness in your eyes, something in your mind that still blocks the true light of Christ from coming through. Again, this is an inside job, and only you can submit yourself to the cleansing power of the blood of our dear Lord and Savior Jesus Christ. When that light shines brightly as God intends, I will be the first to know it, and my joy will be great. You are my beautiful husband, perfect as God created you. This I do see clearly. Let the Holy Spirit wash away any obstruction, let every obstacle become a life-giving opportunity. Don't worry about me. I will be there. "If you don't know me by now, you may never know me!"

    I love you, Sweetheart. You are the man God promised to me. You are my "Dark Thief," a Worthy Vessel for the Spirit of God to indwell. Invite Him in. He'll do the rest.

Johnny Ellis #374452

Johnny Ellis #374452

FEBRUARY, 2001

Hi, Sweetheart! Be my Valentine!

Sunday, February 11, 2001
    I write today, according to the will of God Most High, by the power of the Holy Spirit, in the name of our Lord and Savior Jesus the Christ. You asked for a special letter, a nice letter. Since I can't read your mind and deliver exactly what you want, I let the Holy Spirit guide my words, so you may receive exceedingly, abundantly above anything you could ask or imagine.
    Imagine your thoughts to be like the sunshine, shining over the whole world. Now take a magnifying glass, and focus on one thought. What happens? You start a fire. Sweetheart, I hear your thoughts reflecting what you hear from the people around you, their fears and doubts.
    Now, can you remember, as a child in school, how different you were from your cousins, how much smarter you were, how much easier the school work was for you to accomplish? Project that thought to the present time, and see the Choice Program as school. Sure, it's hard for the others, but know that for you it will be a piece of cake! All you have to do is to focus your attention on your success. See yourself flying through the program eating up every obstacle and converting it into opportunity for your success. Does this make sense to you? I tell you the truth, inspired by the Holy Spirit of God. I know that you know this is true.
    Honey, am I not your barometer? More and more I realize how exquisitely sensitive I am to you. This can mean simply taking my hands off of you if you choose a negative path. Or it will mean that you have the most responsive woman in the universe who will be able to satisfy your every desire. Take your pick. I have made my choice. I'm going to stick with you all the way. I repeat, if you choose the world, you choose to remove me from your life. If you choose the path of righteousness, there I am, ready, willing and able to create a life of beauty, power, and joy with you, my Love.
    Just think about it. Focus on the life that you want, and it will manifest. If you come out of prison, and jump back on the streets, I will know that you have made that choice, and I will let go of you.
    I know that God will provide for me. If you won't be my true

Johnny Ellis #374452

husband, God Himself will come down from heaven and love me. He's already doing it! He wants to love me through you, His Worthy Vessel. Begin to thrill to His Presence in you. Begin to feel what God feels, think what God thinks, do what God does. That's why He created us...to have a means to expand Himself. We are that expansion.

I am fully aware that my love for you is Divine Love flowing through me. During our last visit, I noticed the power of our love building, growing stronger. It's not that the Love itself was increasing, but the manifestation of it was happening. Our Love is so great it will take eternity to begin to express it, to manifest it. We are only tasting it now. There is so much more. You are on the right path, Honey. Use every moment to enforce that path. Let go of every thought that is negative, doubtful, fearful, and replace it with "I can do all things through Christ who strengthens me." Be all that God created you to be. Be my Valentine today and throughout all eternity...my Lover, my Friend, my Partner, my ALL.

I love you, Sweetheart. Nothing will ever change that. Choose to be with me only, and not the filth of the world, and I will always be there for you. We have only just begun the life that God has planned for us.

Thursday, February 15, 2001

Hi, Sweetheart! While rummaging through some old papers, I came across this little story that I wrote down while we were living in the trailer in Wisconsin. I'd like to share it with you now. I hope you enjoy it.

Rose's Fairy Tale

Once there was a girl named Rose. God Himself had named her, for she belonged to Him alone. She had come from His Heart. Living in the world, she had forgotten who she was and lost her way. But, God never once took His eyes off of her.

As a child, Rose would often look into a mirror and see herself as a beautiful bride. This was her favorite fantasy, seeing herself with a crown and veil and a long white dress. One day, Rose became conscious of the wish that had been in her heart all along.

"I want to be God's wife and serve Him all my life." Her

Johnny Ellis #374452

conscious mind was shocked at such a lofty desire. But, there it was, plain as day, written right across her heart.

Now that her great love for God had entered her consciousness, strange and wonderful changes began to happen in Rose's life. God slowly began to reveal Himself to her, for it was He who had put this desire into her heart from the very beginning of time. "Close your eyes and reach out for my hand," said God, "and I will guide you along the pathway that will bring us together. You do not know my ways, and cannot yet understand my plan, but your faith is strong and your love for Me is pure, so you cannot fail in the mission I have assigned you."

As in all fairy tales, Rose was to be the beautiful princess who would kiss a frog who would turn into a handsome prince...or...no...she was to be locked away in a tower and let down her hair for her beloved to climb...or...no...she was to fall asleep for many years and be awakened by the kiss of her beloved...Yes! That's it. Rose's consciousness was asleep, and the Prince kissed her sweetly, and...oh no, that's still not it. No. Now Holy Spirit guide my pen:

Rose, eyes closed, and hand outstretched, is guided by the Spirit of her beloved into the darkness of the night, where great danger is lurking. Protected by the armor of Love, she is led to a man who also has forgotten who he is and lost his way. Filled with God's grace, Rose takes the man's hand and God begins to lead them both out of the darkness. But the man is a prisoner of the darkness and it is no easy task to free him. But with love, faith and a pure heart, Rose causes the scales to begin to fall from the man's eyes, and he starts to see for the first time.

Slowly and tediously he is freed from his entanglement in the darkness. God has allowed a great love to come into Rose's heart for this man, and with this love and patience, and God's protection, Rose stays by his side while the struggle for his freedom goes on. Finally, brought into the light, free at last from all entanglements, this man has eyes to see and ears to hear, and turns to God to know his purpose. immediately the Spirit of Rose's beloved enters into the man and Rose stands face to face with her Bridegroom.

A great Wedding Feast is prepared and all in the Kingdom are invited. Rose is dressed in her real crown, veil and white dress and presented to her Groom. All the people are happy to see the

Johnny Ellis #374452

love between Rose and her Husband. The celebration begins and they all live happily ever after!
   I love you Honey.

Johnny Ellis #374452

MARCH, 2001

I love you. I love your letters. I love your scriptures. I love your love for me and God. I love your strength. I love your willingness to follow Spirit. I love that you are God's man. I love that you are my man! I love that God brought me to you. I love that we are one. I love that God is working in our lives in such a wonderful way to show His glory. I love that we are growing young and healthy, heart, soul, mind, and body. I love that God continually blesses us and leads us in the right path, according to His Will.

Friday, March 16, 2001

Hi Sweetie!
    The above paragraph is an excerpt from my letter to you of December 22, 1999. I awoke very early the other morning, and got up intending to write you a letter. Instead, I began reading what I had already written. It seems evident that you have been taking my letters into your heart and mind, where they have been working to heal you, to strengthen you, and to lead you to a closer walk with the Lord. Thank God that I have had this opportunity to love you and share God's love with you.
    I'll write more later. I love you.

Tuesday, March 20, 2001

Hi, Sweetie!
    I took the King! Our new bed will be delivered next Friday. It's been such a long time since I've slept in a real bed, I'm happy. This is the bed I will share with my true husband, a husband who will not defile me or our marriage bed with his thoughts, words, or deeds, but will be true to God and to me, his wife. This is the only husband that I want, the man that God has promised to me.
    If you are not that man, say so now. Do not try to deceive me any further. You cannot serve God and the world. You cannot be my husband and still lust after other women. If there is any doubt in your mind that you will be faithful to me, get out of my life now. I will no longer tolerate your filthy behavior. You will no longer infect me with the filth of the world. That time is over. I'm perfectly

Johnny Ellis #374452

happy and contented to share my bed with the Spirit of God. If that spirit does not live in you completely, stop your correspondence to me now.

Wow, where did that come from? I wanted to share the good news of the bed with you, and out comes my doubt and fear, mixed with a little anger. Well, it's time I stand up for myself. I accepted you just as you were when I met you, because you didn't have the Word in you. But you do now, so you can make the choice to go all the way with God, or all the way with the world. The Holy Spirit won't let you fool me now, so don't even try. I do love you, but I can live without you.

Wednesday, March 21, 2001

Hi, Honey!

Happy Spring! We know that our marriage has not had a solid foundation. We know that from the beginning you told me many lies. We know that you still desired other women, and willingly had relations with them. We know that it's time for us to start over. It's time for you to decide if you really want to be married to me. It's time for you to propose to me, if that is your desire. It's time for us to plan our future. It's time, if you really want me to be your wife, and to love me as Christ loves the Church, for us to plan a wedding.

Let me say this, John. I do love you with a Godly love. Even if you do not want to be married to me, I will still be your friend. I will help you to start a new life in whatever way I can. You married me under the influence of drugs and alcohol. Now, with a clear mind, you are free to choose again. I will not hold you to anything you agreed to while under the influence. I give you the gift of freedom. Search you heart, soul, and mind. I don't want a lukewarm husband, or a part-time man that must be shared with others. If you aren't ready to make a total commitment to me in marriage, I understand. Let's be friends in Christ. He must have charge of our lives. He will lead us in the right path, together or separately.

Looking back over these ten years, I haven't felt like a bride. I certainly haven't been a priority in your life. You have always had another agenda going on in your life. So, if we end it, I certainly will not be missing much. It's not like you once adored

Johnny Ellis #374452

me and put me on a pedestal that I must now give up. Life can only get better with or without you. I'm through suffering. By the grace of God I lived through this time with you. But now I'm ready for glory after glory. I won't settle for less. We are both free.

Johnny Ellis #374452

Johnny Ellis #374452

APRIL, 2001

Monday, April 2, 2001

Hi Sweetheart,
　　My life has truly become glorious, and I claim glory after glory. John, the Bible only contains a little bit of what Jesus said and did. As the Apostle John stated, if it was all written down, the world could not contain all the books. But when we look to Him as our teacher and our guide, He reveals more and more to us each moment.
　　Let go of all limitations, and trust Him always in all ways. Look to Him to do for you everything you feel unable to do for yourself. Soon you will merge with the Christ and be filled with all power. John, this is God's plan for all of His children, not just for Jesus. He came to show us the Way. He came to reconnect us to the Spirit of God and to awaken us to our own Divinity. He's not through with us.
　　Be in the world but not of it. Though your body is in prison, keep you heart, soul, and mind united with God. Never allow this connection to be broken. That's where free will comes in. You must make this your conscious choice at all times.
　　Here's a picture of my new King. You will have to use your imagination to put the bodies in it. May God continue to bless you, strengthen you and bring you into perfect harmony with His will for you in all you think, say, and do. I love you a lot, but not half as much as when you are whole.

Thursday evening, April 5, 2001

Hi, Sweetie!

　　The joy of the Lord is our strength. We can do all things through Christ Who strengthens us. He is building us up. Have no doubt. To doubt is of the devil. Let the Holy Spirit of God give you the words to say when it's time to tell of your experience. Confess the Word, John, not the lies of the world.
　　Time for my King. I'll write more tomorrow. I love you, Sweetie.

Johnny Ellis #374452

Hi Honey!

It's early Friday morning and I've just been reading the Book of James. He gives a good description of doubt. James 1:6 ....*he who doubts is like a wave of the sea driven and tossed by the wind.* In Hebrews 3:12 we are told to *beware, lest there be in you an evil heart of unbelief.*

If you have faith and do not doubt...you may say to this mountain, "Be removed and be cast into the sea," and it will be done. And all things whatever you ask in prayer, believing, you will receive. Matthew 21:22. (But unbelief will prevent it.)

Again I say to you that if two of you agree on earth concerning anything that they ask, it will be done for them by My Father in heaven. For where two or three are gathered together in My name, I am there in the midst of them. Matthew 18:19-20. We two have asked. We two receive in the name of Jesus. In Matthew 14:31 Jesus said to Peter as he sunk in the water, *Oh you of little faith, why did you doubt?* But to the woman of Canaan, who cried out to him to have mercy on her severely demon-possessed daughter, he said, *O woman, great is your faith! Let it be to you as you desire. And her daughter was healed from that very hour.* Matthew 15:28.

Jesus was rejected in his home town of Nazareth. *And He did not do many mighty works there because of their unbelief.* Matthew 13:58. We also hear Jesus saying, *As you have believed, so let it be done for you. Be of good cheer, daughter; your faith has made you well. According to you faith let it be to you.* We can't miss!

Tuesday, April 17, 2001

Hi Sweetie!

I received your card and your letter last night when I got home from a full day. Thank you very much. Just a few days ago, I wrote a poem about the Lord's little lamb, so your card is truly precious to me.

> Sweet Jesus, I am your little lamb.
> You hold me in Your hand.
> Your love flows over me
> For everyone to see.

Johnny Ellis #374452

You'll never let me go.
Now the whole world knows
That I'm Your little lamb!

Move Mountain
Move mountain. Be cast into the sea.
I have no time to mess with thee.
You came from the world where **change** is the rule.
I'm hooked to the eternal. I'm no fool.
So move mountain. Be on your merry way.
I have a Sweet Lord of Love to serve today.

I'm sure Jesus is guiding all the events that occur for you. Stay conscious of His presence, and His hand in all that transpires. Remember O.O.O. and greet every obstacle as an opportunity to grow. I plan to see you tomorrow, Wednesday. I do love you, and I keep that love in the Lord's hands, for Him to direct.

Friday, April 27, 2001

Hi Sweetie Pie!
Thank you for sharing the story of the Lily with me. Let me tell you about my Lily!

Lonely Rose
There was a Rose, a very sad and lonely Rose.
She'd lean upon the garden wall,
And she'd call
Out to God in pain:
Oh hear my prayer. I need to share,
As I need sun and rain.
And then one day, a lovely lily grew her way.
He was the fairest flower of all,
Straight and tall,
Pure as new fall'n snow.
God heard her prayer, and he was there
For her alone to know.

Are you my Lily? Are you the one God brought up out of

Johnny Ellis #374452

the miry clay, out of the filth at the bottom of the pond, especially to be mine? Are you my own husband? Am I your own wife? God created marriage to be an exclusive relationship. Why should we settle for less than God's best? I won't. No husband of mine will ever lust after another woman. My husband's desire is for me alone.

My husband knows that I am a virtuous wife. To him my worth is far above rubies. His heart safely trusts me. He will have no lack of gain. I do him good all the days of my life. I open my mouth with wisdom, and on my tongue is the law of kindness. My children rise up and call me blessed. My husband also, and he praises me, because I am a woman who loves the Lord. (Proverbs 31)

And the Lord God said, "It is not good that Johnny Louis Ellis should be alone. I will bring him a helper comparable to him." The Lord God brought His very own Rose to be Johnny's wife. Is this not a wonder? You must have done something very good to deserve to have me as your wife. Hmmm. I wonder what it was? Do you have a clue?

Are you staying in His Word. Are you confessing God's blessings every day? Don't neglect God. Stay mindful of God in all you do. He is doing a mighty work in you and me. The world is so hungry for what we will bring in the name of Love.

You said it's better to be faithful than famous. We know that God does exceedingly, abundantly above anything we can think, ask or imagine. We'll have it all...faith, fame, wealth, because we seek first the Kingdom of God and His righteousness. He will not hold back any good thing from us. Of course the greatest gift he has given us is the Gift of Himself, and the gift of each other, you for me, and me for you. Are you ready for all He has prepared for us? All we must do is hear and obey. I love you.

Johnny Ellis #374452

MAY, 2001

Tuesday, May 1, 2001

To My Precious Husband,
    Oh, God is a great God, a God of goodness and mercy. In the Choice Program, your spirit was growing deeper into the darkness. That program is based on the ignorance of man, which is darkness. Do not seek this darkness. Stay in His Word.
    John, what a difference. Our visits were repelling me while you were in that program. You were filling yourself, the vessel of God, with darkness, and I could feel it, as well as hear it in all your words. What a relief for me that you are back in His Word. When your light shines as it did on our last visit, Sunday, my whole being vibrates with joy and love. Then you don't need to tell me that you are My Husband, because it flows from every cell of your body, attracting me to you, drawing me into you, merging us into the oneness for which we were created.
    Today is the first of May. May is our month, the month that God gave us birth, to come into the world to do His will, for His purpose alone. All that we have experienced to this day is being purified and refined into our testimony. We must fill ourselves with His light, the light of His Word. Then our lights will merge, and shine into the world of darkness, freeing all the prisoners of the darkness. Where is the darkness when the light shines into it? Even a child can answer this question. What an easy job, what a joy, just to go around the world letting our light shine.
    This is the job God is calling us to, John. Can you imagine what it is like? As we feed the hungry souls with His Truth, we bring healing, and we bring Heaven, His Kingdom to the earth. That's our job, Honey! Stay in His Word. Get His Word into your belly, let it permeate every fiber of your being. When we are filled with His Light, there is no darkness in us. Hence, there is no sickness, fault, blame, misery, etc. in us. We are free to be all that God created us to be. I claim this life for us in the Mighty Name of Jesus, Who paid the price so that we may live.
    The Lord is showing me that we should be together today, so I will cut this letter short. Yes, I received your voice message yesterday. "This is your Husband." The words thrilled me. I saved it so I could hear it over and over. I'll never tire of hearing your

Johnny Ellis #374452

words of love. They are food for my heart, soul, and spirit.
So, my darling love, let me prepare myself for our meeting. God has filled me with a Love Divine especially for you. I love everyone, but, the part of me that is a wife, and that is every bit of me, God has given to you. He chose us to be together before the foundation of the earth. His will is eternal, as is our love for each other. I am yours. You are mine. We are His, in the name of Jesus. Amen. I love you, Sweetie!

Friday, May 11, 2001

Hi, Honey!
Happy Birthday to you, my Love. God blessed the world the day you were born. *He Himself gave some to be...teachers, for the equipping of the saints, for the work of ministry, for the edifying of the body of Christ.* Ephesians 4:11-12

I'm Gonna Teach the Word

I'm gonna teach the word,
The word God gave to me.
He taught me what we gotta do
So we can all be free.

He taught me what I gotta say
So you will notice me there.
He even taught me how to dress,
And how to wear my hair.

And now he sent my lovin' man
To stand here by my side.
Together we will take a stand
And wipe out racial pride.

Yes, God gives me all I need.
That's why I work for Him.
He's set me up in business.
I move with vigor and vim.

The world's gonna love me,

Johnny Ellis #374452

> The entire human race
> When I bring Jesus home to meet you.
> I've already seen His face.
>
> He never really left us.
> We've just been too blind to know.
> But soon He will reveal Himself.
> We all will feel His glow!

I copied this poem from my manuscript. I wanted to share it with you at this time. My wish for every human being on the planet is for each one to discover their true self, the person that God created them to be. Of course, this is my wish for you. We must look within to discover who we are. Have you been looking? Remember, *seek and you will find.* I know that God wants you by my side as I step out. I'm not meant to step out onto the world stage without you, except to prepare the way for you. Take that journey within now, while you have the time, and make the most wonderful discovery of your life. Discover who God created you to be. Then you will be ready to join me and bless the world.

Happy Birthday. I love you!

Thursday, May 17, 2001

Hi, Honey!

It's very early in the morning, 4:39 a.m. to be exact, and I'm wide awake. So I will take this opportunity to write to you, even though I will be seeing you soon.

John, I'm being so blessed by these Kenneth Hagin Bible Study Courses that you sent home. I like them much more than the correspondence courses I have been taking. The book on Faith is really powerful. Hagin takes the Truth of God's Word and makes it so simple, using his personal experience to bring it to life. I just praise God and thank Him for Kenneth Hagin. What a sweet, precious soul he is!

In Isaiah 43:25 God says, *I, even I, am he that blotteth out thy transgressions ...and will not remember thy sins.* Hagin says <u>once we confess a sin, we must not keep confessing the same sins over and over again because that only builds weakness, doubt, and sin-consciousness into our spirit</u>. If you confessed your

Johnny Ellis #374452

sin once, God forgave you and He forgot it, so you need to forget it. God has no memory of your sin once you truly repent and ask for forgiveness. (The "Choice" program builds sin-consciousness!)   I love you Honey.

Friday, May 25, 2001

Hi Sweetheart!
    How I love looking into your eyes. We have a very real soul connection.
    Honey, I've been reading Kenneth Hagin's book on faith, and I'm really getting it. He keeps repeating Mark 11:23-24. *For assuredly, I say to you, whoever says to this mountain, "Be removed and be cast into the sea," and does not doubt in his heart, but believes that those things he says will come to pass, he will have whatever he says. Therefore I say to you, whatever things you ask when you pray, believe that you receive them, and you will have them."*
    Believe. Receive. Nothing can keep us apart when we believe. I love you.

Johnny Ellis #374452

JUNE, 2001

Sunday, June 3, 2001

My Dear, Sweet Husband,
Our visit yesterday was truly Divine! Honey, you are my true husband. I enjoyed your presence on every level. Your spirit was completely present in your body. Spirit knows no boundaries, and your spirit also was fully present with me all night through. Every cell of my body was awakened. Our love is truly Divine. We One! And, we won! We have broken through every barrier. We have perfect Oneness, heart, soul, mind and body.

Saturday, June 9, 2001

Hi Sweetie,
Our visits are becoming more beautiful each time. I really believe we're "getting it." We're catching on to God's plan for us. We are bringing out the best in each other. Together we'll bring out the best in the world. When we see each person as the image of God, our "seeing" brings that out in the person. We can do this one on one, and we can accomplish this before thousands or even millions of people.
Truly, I remember when Kevin was just a little guy, and he told me, "Mom, I just figured something out. God is all powerful, and everything is His. So He really doesn't care if we ask Him for a penny or for a million dollars. It's all the same to Him. So why waste our time asking for a penny. Let's go for the million!"
I'm going for the million. Together we can change the world. Let's continue to practice our perfect harmony, our Divine Love for each other. This kind of love has no limits, and as we receive it from God, we are filled to overflowing so that it touches all that we come in contact with.
But always remember, we one. Male and female He made us. We are a couple, man and wife. So while we allow agape love to flow to all humanity, our sexual union is sacred just between you and me. We have each other not only to satisfy every need, but to continually thrill each other, lifting us to higher and higher levels of joy and ecstasy. Sweetheart, as this sinks in, we are unlimited in the amount of God power that flows through us to

Johnny Ellis #374452

each other, and to all the world.
    You are my true partner. Of this there is no doubt. Our certainty is the source of our power. As we look into each other's eyes, we can begin to see eternity. As we seek first the Kingdom of God and His righteousness, we tap into the source of all goodness, all beauty, all truth, all joy, all prosperity, all perfection, exceedingly, abundantly above all that we can ask, think, or imagine. This is the life we have chosen when we asked God to choose our partner. He answered your prayer by sending me to you, just as He chose you for me. We truly are a marriage made in Heaven.
    I love you, Johnny Louis Ellis. You are the only man for me. Together we blossom and grow, and the beauty of our love for each other lights the world.

And they started to dance like old lovers who know and cherish each other's grace; and his arm never pushed or pulled her, and her eyes never left his face

Tuesday, June 12, 2001

Hi, Sweetheart,
    The above quote was shared by a woman at a "Love & Action" luncheon. When I heard it, it really touched my heart. It depicts the beautiful relationship of two people who know each other intimately and completely. It's another way of saying, "We One!" This is the relationship that we have both longed for. And God has brought us together for just this experience.

Thursday, June 14, 2001

Hi again!
    Our visit yesterday was phenomenal! Darling, looking into your eyes was amazing. You literally filled me up with love and strength. I felt a little tired driving there, but after our visit, I was completely revitalized! You're better than coffee!! I'll have you anytime! Your looking into my eyes as you prayed was beyond anything I have ever experienced in my life. John, we are discovering new frontiers in relationship. What a joy and wonder our love is!

Johnny Ellis #374452

Tuesday, June 19, 2001

Dear John,
 Just as I was told in my vision, healing love flows between us when we gaze into each other's eyes. Now we can only imagine the rest of the vision, being truly "one" heart, soul, mind, and body, but, for now, three out of four is not bad!
 I see I've reached the bottom of the page. Sweetheart, all of our communication is good, whether we are eye to eye, heart to heart, soul to soul, body to body. It's all good. I praise and thank the Lord for all we have. Soon we will have it ALL! I love you.

Johnny Ellis #374452

Johnny Ellis #374452

AUGUST, 2001

Wednesday, August 1, 2001

Hi Sweetie!
    I see that it's quite a while since I wrote a "real" letter to you, although we have been communicating on a higher level meanwhile. Our eye contact as we pray is so satisfying to me. It calms my soul. It truly is a short-cut to building trust between us.
    I am beginning to "see" things so clearly now. I realize that for everything God has a divine plan. Our part is to tap into it with our consciousness. We must keep our mind focused on God, on Divine guidance, every moment. Whenever we forget, and begin to follow our "own" thoughts, usually garbage picked up from the environment, we get off track. When we "put on the mind of Christ," we are connected to the Divine plan, and rise above the world's ways. To me, this is the ONLY WAY to live. Everything else is worthless nonsense.
    It's time to set a new standard for life. We know that there is a way in the world that seems right, but the end of it is death. We must demonstrate a new way of thinking, a new way of being in this world, in it, but not of it. Of course, for Jesus, this is nothing new, but, for the rest of us, it is a brand new experience. I believe that I am demonstrating the truth of His words in my life, and creating a new standard that others will be able to follow. I have become a doer of the Word, and my life has reached new levels of joy and excitement. Sweet surprises wait around every corner. That open mind that you spoke of is the key to new discovery. And when we seek the highest Truth, all that we discover is of the highest Good, real God substance!
    Since you got out of "Choice" last time, our marriage has really grown. The "marriage enrichment" seminars have been a great help. God bless Sharon and Al. They are doing a great job. I believe we have many new insights into what makes a marriage. May our love for each other and our marriage relationship continue to blossom and grow throughout eternity.
    Even though you are back in the Choice Program, when you keep your heart, soul, mind, and strength focused on the Lord and His Word, you will be setting a new standard for the program. We know that all things work together for good when you love God

and are called according to His purpose. Train yourself to "see" with your spiritual eyes all that God has for you every moment. And continue to develop your spiritual ears so that you will continuously "hear" His voice guiding you moment by moment into the path of righteousness, the only way to go. We go that way together. I love you.

Sunday Night, August 26, 2001

Hi, Sweetheart,

    Are you my Spirit Lover? Did my love draw you to me in the flesh? I love you, Honey. Good night, my Love, Partner, High Priest, Beloved, Joy of my Life, Precious Angel, and so much more...........

Johnny Ellis #374452

SEPTEMBER, 2001

Saturday morning, September 1, 2001

Hi Daddy!
    Here are some poems I wrote about my Spirit Lover back in the '80's. They fit you so very well. Today they are dedicated to you, Johnny Louis Ellis, my Love.

Come, I will show you the bride, the Lamb's wife.
Revelation 21:9

The One Who Loves Me

There is one special man Made just for me.
As soon as He finds me His partner I'll be.

He sees me as perfect. He loves every part.
And so He's reserved A place in His heart

Where He carries my picture So when we meet,
He's sure to recognize His love so sweet.

Yes, I am His love, And so I'll be true.
I'll wait till He finds me When we will renew

The love that's been burning Forever inside.
He'll come and He'll claim me. Yes, I am His bride!

I will give you a new heart and put a new spirit within you.
Ezekiel 36:26

Fidelity

Fidelity He's asked of me,
To save the part Within my heart
Made for my mate. So I will wait.

But I'm not alone. He's made himself known.
He reaches me With His spirit free.

Johnny Ellis #374452

>His presence is real. His love I feel.
>
>It's up to me A woman to be
>Who knows her own will. I will wait until
>He's standing before me. Oh, He will adore me!
>
>I'm saving myself for marriage!
>Praise God!!

Yes, on that November night back in 1990, did you not recognize your true love? Did you not know without reservation that I was yours, that I belonged only to you, totally? Did you not claim me for your own? And did I not respond with my whole being?

And now, we are ready for the fulfillment of God's plan for our union, our holy partnership. We have put on the mind of Christ. We are through with the nonsense of the world, anger, sickness, all sorts of foolishness. We step into the Perfection of God. We are the image of God, male and female He made us, one flesh, one heart, one soul, one mind, one with God and one with each other. We Won! We One!.

I love you.

Johnny Ellis #374452

OCTOBER, 2001

Monday, October 1, 2001

Hi Honey,

Wow! I can hardly believe that a whole month has passed since I wrote you a real letter. But, in a way, I have already said all there is to say. I have expressed my love for you in every way I could imagine. Words are no longer adequate.

And God is telling us, "You ain't seen nothin' yet!" Two people in harmony with God are in harmony with each other. That's why we put God FIRST! We love Him with our whole heart, soul, mind, and strength (body). I have no doubt that our marriage will be like no other.

I love that you get hard when you pray in tongues. I go into ecstasy. Can you imagine when we are together in the flesh what it will be like? No, you can't imagine. Eye has not seen, ear has not heard what He has prepared for us because we love Him. He is doing exceedingly, abundantly above and beyond anything we can imagine.

You know that when you talk "Scripture" to me how it excites me. Just try to imagine us together, alone, naked, between the sheets, speaking in tongues! Now, whatever you imagine, multiply it a thousand times, and then ten thousand times, and still we can't imagine how it will be.

All we can do for now is cement our relationship to God. The rest will take care of itself. Just love God 24/7. Continuously seek His will. Yes, it is His will for us to love each other. I believe that we are Divine Lovers, Krisna and Radharani. We are united heart, soul, and mind. Nothing can separate us. The physical is our reward for our faithfulness to God. It is His gift to us.

We had it once. Do you see how you threw it away? Do you know what went wrong? Are you doing all that you can to remove the cause of our separation? I believe that you are. And I believe that the Holy Spirit of God is assisting you in every way. Be ever mindful of Divine guidance and help pouring into your heart, your renewed mind, every cell of your body. Know that we won. We one. Nothing can tear us apart.

Believe. Receive. All things are possible to him who believes. Believe in perfect health, believe in eternal life, without

Johnny Ellis #374452

limitations. What Godly purpose do limitations serve? Limitations are from the devil. Remove disease and death from your vocabulary. Give up the pain of the past and the fear of the future. This moment is eternity. When we live fully in this moment, we are in eternal life, in this body, NOW! It is true. The truth makes us free, free from the lies and limitations of Satan's world. We need to go all the way with God. John, when you understand this, you will really be free. No walls will be able to hold you. The only thing God wants to hold you is my arms!

Honey, I'm making the most of my life while you are there, but my life will really begin when we are together. You are the spark that lights my fire. I will pile up the lumber in the fire place, but the real flame of love will burst forth when we are together. I know this is true. Nothing can compare to me and you! Together!

As we speak in tongues, the bridge is being built between our lives. I love you.

Johnny Ellis #374452

DECEMBER, 2001

Indeed I have spoken it; I will also bring it to pass. I have purposed it; I will also do it. Isaiah 46:11

Friday, December 28, 2001

Hi Honey,
    While sorting through some books, I came across the following prophecy which I received from the Lord and I wrote down on May 2, 1994:

According to the will of God Most High, in the Name of our Lord and Savior Jesus Christ, by the Power of the Holy Spirit, I seek a word today from the Lord for John and me.

Beloved,
    Know that I am with you always in all ways. You are a precious pair to me. Your light will shine for all the world to see. Yes, you are the ultimate "in love" couple. You will show the meaning of love to the world in your actions, by your v e r y being. I bless you with a Love Divine, eternal and true, that never can be broken. You are the pair that will free the world of illusion and misery, and bring peace and joy over all. The crooked will be made straight through my love and power flowing through you.
    You will travel the world in My Name, shining the light of My Glory over all. Your smiles will light the material sky and shine away all illusions. What remains will be heaven on earth, the Kingdom so long ago promised to the nations. You are the key to unlock the plan of salvation for all of my children.
    Bless you and be at peace knowing that you are no longer a part of the world, but rather you are My emissaries bringing the good news to all of My beloved people. Be one forever. Lord Jesus Christ

    This came through nearly eight years ago! God is certainly patient with us. But, His Will is eternal. I believe this is His Plan. So, any time you're ready, so am I.
    Right now I keep seeing the Risen Christ with holes in His hands and side. This clearly demonstrates that He did not look at Himself, or circumstances. He kept His thoughts at One with the

Johnny Ellis #374452

Father. He teaches us by His example. All physical symptoms are simply to be ignored, overlooked. Only then can we truly be Overcomers, rising above the world to the glory God has prepared for us from the beginning of time.

    Another year is passing away. Soon it will be 2002. What wonders will God manifest in our lives now? Like Jesus walking to the cross, bleeding, weary, we keep our heart, souls, mind and strength fixed on God the Father. He will bring us through. He has given us each other. He loves us through one another. I love you.

Johnny Ellis #374452

Johnny Ellis #374452

Johnny Ellis #374452

ADDENDUM

Johnny's Re-Entry Story
Reprinted from
"The First Twenty-Nine Days: Twenty True Stories of Re-Entry"

    I had hoped to be able to return to Illinois upon my release, but found out I was mandated to Madison, where the offense was committed. I wanted to get out of Wisconsin. I felt I had paid my debt.
    My last week in prison, tension was building. I felt like I was suspect, as if I was going to steal a fork or a roll of toilet paper. They were treating me like a criminal! I had to dig deep to remember all the principles I had learned in the Bible and "Anger Management."
    I had decided to dedicate my life to Christ more than four years earlier after the judge said, "Bailiff, cuff him!" Click, click, and I was off to the county jail cell. My world had come to an end. I was suffering from withdrawals from numerous addictions to heroin, methadone, cocaine, marijuana, alcohol, cigarettes, and sex—a long tunnel with no escape, an abyss.
    Just before heading out for Dodge Correctional Institution, another inmate handed me a Gideon Bible. That was the only possession allowed to be carried on the bus going to my new home at Dodge. I somehow knew that there was power in that Book to change my life, if only I could dedicate my life to it.

Day One

    Tuesday is the day felons are released from prison all over Wisconsin. My out date was Tuesday, February 17, 2004. I had no idea what to expect. The night before, I was packing my stuff too slowly to please the guards, so they set me out of the cell and literally threw everything into a box and taped it shut. The next morning I had to repack everything.
    I decided to wear my sweatpants and shirt. I was brought to the gatehouse and told to change clothes. What a surprise! I had no idea that Rose had gone to the Community Thrift Store and bought a complete outfit for me, including shoes and leather jacket. Everything fit perfectly. I was elated.

Johnny Ellis #374452

I was disappointed that Rose was not allowed to pick me up. I was picked up by a Corrections driver. Two women from the women's prison were also picked up. I looked so good in my new clothes, the women thought I was a guard, and started asking me questions. The driver took me to the bank so I could cash the check for $440 with my prison ID. I began to plan ahead knowing that I would soon have to pay rent, and buy food; $440 would not go very far.

I had been told that I would need a leg bracelet. I explained to the driver that I had neuropathy, a condition that affected the circulation in my feet. When he said, "Let's go," I asked, "What about the bracelet?" He replied, "You're not getting one!" I knew immediately that this was the favor of God, and I silently thanked the Lord.

I had heard about the program where we are mandated to spend our first twenty-nine days in a hotel. I was brought to the "Expo," a hot spot for people in the life, complete with drug dealers and prostitutes. And it was only a few blocks from where my crime had been committed. I felt like I was being set up to fail and get thrown back in jail. I had to consciously get into the right mind frame, take a deep breath, and tap into my inner guidance to find the strength to resist any temptations that were coming my way.

The Corrections officer signed me into the hotel and gave me my instructions to report to my parole officer within three days and see what she required. I settled down and suddenly realized that I was free to walk outside, go to the store, and even spend some money! I got some change and called my Baby. I told her the good news that I was free. "How soon can you get here?" "As soon as the sun comes up!" I gave her directions. Thus ended my first day of freedom.

Day Two

The next day, dressed in my "new" clothes, I stepped out of my room. The first person I saw said to me, "Are you lookin'?" I said, "What?" He repeated, "Are you lookin' to score?" I answered, "I already did. I've got Jesus!" "Yeah, okay man, I'm gone!" He nearly ran from me. The Word came to my remembrance, "Resist the devil and he will flee!" Thank God for His Word.

Johnny Ellis #374452

I headed for the store, and, to my surprise, there she was driving towards me, earlier than expected. I was coming back into a new world. I found myself evaluating everything. When I saw my Baby, I knew my prayer was answered and all my stress and long suffering would be relieved. For the first time in more than four years, we were alone together ... no guards, no rules, no inhibitions.

During our time together we telephoned my parole officer and set up a meeting for the next day. Rose got the impression that my P.O. expected her to come with me. We held hands and prayed together that God would grant us favor and touch and prepare the heart of my P.O. so that she would allow me to have an interstate pass to be able to spend some time with my Baby in Illinois.

The bewitching hour of 10 P.M. came all too soon, and we had to say "good bye". My greatest temptation was to keep her with me overnight. A few hours were not enough to satisfy the love and passion that had welled up inside of me for her. It was hard when I let her go, but rules are rules. I watched TV until the wee hours, when finally I dozed off. I was excited that my Baby would be back the next day, and by my side when I would present myself to my new P.O. for the first time. I had no idea what to expect, but we were confident that God had it all under control. I remembered the Scripture, Psalm 50:15: "Call on me in your day of trouble, and I will deliver you."

Day Three

Finally morning came, and so did she, with a bright smile and the look of victory on her face, giving glory to God that this would be the day that we would ride off together to a new horizon, over the borderline. We greeted each other, and confidently agreed that we were going to receive our blessing and favor from the Lord.

We arrived at the parole office and were greeted with a smile, unexpected from a parole officer! We felt in our spirit that Carrie was special. To our delight she proved to be nothing less. During our dialogue, I shared with her some of my strengths and weaknesses and my goals and desires. She expressed that she was pleased that I was open and honest with her. She was glad to

Johnny Ellis #374452

see that I had someone very supportive who made it her business to be with me at every turn regardless of the distance. Rose had traveled many miles to see me during my incarceration, and she wasn't ready to slow down yet.

We were hoping to be granted a few days together in Illinois. We were surprised with a travel permit for fourteen days, the maximum Carrie could allow under the circumstances. We were amazed and excited. Rumor had it that it would be impossible to get an interstate permit after less than a week of supervision. But what is impossible for man is possible for God. It was all we could do to hold back the joy and exhilaration we felt. It seemed like we had just been touched by an angel. We thanked Carrie and said goodbye. We returned to the hotel where I quickly grabbed some things. We hit the road, thanking and praising God all the way to my Baby's home.

Day Four to Day Eighteen

There we were in our cozy, warm love nest, the comfort of a woman's touch, a real bathtub, a king-sized bed, walking around the Fox River instead of the prison yard. It was a blessing to be able to stay with my Baby where I was able to live comfortably without having to pay any bills. I was able to hold my $440, especially since I was no longer dependent on alcohol, drugs, and cigarettes. Again I thank God for delivering me from all of this.
I had become accustomed to a certain routine while in prison. I was able to maintain the discipline with my Baby. I had walked every day in the prison yard talking to God and thinking of her. Now I could walk with Rose and we could talk to God together, giving Him praise, honor and glory for all that God had already done. He had brought us back together, and God alone was preserving me, keeping me free from bad habits. In prison I had established new ways of living with Christian principles. I was dwelling in the secret place of the Most High. Now my fortress was there with Rose, my secret garden. I was away from the world and its deadly desires. I knew that in the world one is too many and one thousand is never enough because the flesh could never be satisfied. Now I could focus in my spirit and feed it with the Word, which is spiritual food for the soul.

Johnny Ellis #374452

Looking back at this time, I can see clearly how I was being prepared during my incarceration for this new life with my wife. I had walked through the Refiner's fire, and now we were walking together with God. In retrospect, when I entered the prison, I was like a broken pot, fractured, skinny and weak, depleted, lost in a desert. Slowly I realized that both physically and spiritually this was going to be an inside job. I needed to find some new hope, and I did, when Rose sent me a Bible Scripture, Luke 13:6-9. It is a parable of Jesus telling about a certain man with a fig tree planted in his vineyard. The tree did not bear fruit, so he instructed the keeper of the vineyard to "Cut it down; why does it use up the ground?" But the keeper interceded for the fig tree, asking for it to be spared one more year during which time he would dig around it and fertilize it. "And if it bears fruit, well. But if not, after that you can cut it down." The fig tree was given one last chance.

From this parable I fully realized that rather than seeing myself as arrested, I had been rescued, and this was my last chance. I was ready and willing to walk through the fire. The seed had been planted, and the prison became my growing place. Rose and I had begun praying together in the prison visiting room. We would look into each other's eyes while we bared our souls to God. This was and is a powerful experience. To this day, this experience of God's presence in our love continues to strengthen our relationship.

Day Nineteen to Forever

Strengthened by the two weeks with Rose in Illinois, I returned to Madison and my P.O. A few days later, Rose returned to bring me home with her for another fourteen days. This time I had a surprise for her. I showed her my new driver's license. She immediately handed me her car key. She had put on enough miles. She was ready to put me in the driver's seat of her life, as a real husband. God is so good!!!!

Johnny Ellis #374452

Johnny Ellis #374452

POST SCRIPT

Abraham Rose and Johnny L. Ellis Today

Johnny L. Ellis and Abraham Rose, authors, speakers, and spiritual coaches, are co-founders of His Rose, Inc., a Worldwide Spiritual Ministry of Love, Truth and Beauty. "His Rose" is dedicated to raising awareness of spiritual principles through personal testimony and inspired literature, offering "living proof" that God is alive and well, and that His Word is faithful and true.

Today, Johnny is a Minister of Christ as well as a graduate of Madison Media Institute and Grassroots Leadership College. He has completed training with the Industrial Area Foundation (IAF) as a community organizer and is also a registered substance abuse counselor-in-training.

Abraham Rose, spiritual educator, speaker, author, poet, and pianist, is a woman of faith whose life miraculously demonstrates the spiritual principles she shares with her readers and listeners. Her inspirational words have power to transform lives. Just a few words from Abraham Rose have been known to turn lives around and put people on a higher path. Her life is a testament to the power of Divine Love. She has overcome many trials and tribulations, enabling her to help others not just from theory, but real life experience.

Both Johnny and Abraham, graduates of "Toastmasters International," are powerful and charismatic speakers. Their life experiences qualify them as "overcomers" in the true sense of the word, providing hope for others. As ambassadors for God, the authors are stepping out to share their stories and their love with the world. Together they are determined to lead others to realize their God-ordained divine perfection, the true potential of all mankind.

Johnny Ellis #374452

Johnny, I'm Your Woman Now!

Johnny, I'm your woman now!
Somehow
We'll find a way to share eternity.
You're all I have. I'm yours and you belong to me.
Johnny, I'm your woman now.

Johnny, you've shown me the way
To pray.
We've loved before. I can't say where or when.
You couldn't wait to hold me in your arms again.
Johnny, you've shown me the way.

Johnny, we've so much to share.
You care.
You lift me up and make my spirit strong.
Our hearts and souls sing such a lovely song.
Johnny, we've so much to share.

Johnny, I want the world to know
Our glow.
Our love's ablaze. It lights the evening sky...
A beacon bright that others may travel by.
Johnny, I want the world to know!

www.ingramcontent.com/pod-product-compliance
Lightning Source LLC
Chambersburg PA
CBHW071140090426
42736CB00012B/2177